Leading the Transition

Leading the Transition

MANAGEMENT'S ROLE IN CREATING A TEAM-BASED CULTURE

Wilbur L. Pike III

QUALITY RESOURCES®
A Division of The Kraus Organization Limited.
New York, New York

Most Quality Resources books are available at quantity discounts when purchased in bulk. For more information contact:

Special Sales Department
Quality Resources
A Division of The Kraus Organization Limited
902 Broadway
New York, New York 10010
800-247-8519

Copyright © 1995 Wilbur L. Pike III

All rights reserved. No part of this work covered by the copyrights hereon may be reproduced or used in any form or by any means — graphic, electronic, or mechanical, including photocopying, recording, taping, or information storage and retrieval systems — without written permission of the publisher.

Printed in the United States of America

97 96 95   10 9 8 7 6 5 4 3 2 1

Quality Resources
A Division of The Kraus Organization Limited
902 Broadway
New York, New York 10010
800-247-8519

∞

The paper used in this publication meets the minimum requirements of American National Standard for Information Sciences — Permanence of Paper for Printed Library Materials, ANSI Z39.48-1984.

ISBN 0-527-76247-4

Library of Congress Cataloging-in-Publication Data
Pike, Wilbur L.
    Leading the transition : management's role in creating a team-based culture / Wilbur L. Pike.
      p. cm.
  ISBN 0-527-76247-4
  1. Organizational change — Management.   2. Corporate reorganizations — Management.   3. Self-directed work groups.   4. Corporate culture.   I. Title.
HD58.8.P53   1995
858.4′063 — dc20   94-44928
                                                CIP

This book is dedicated to my parents, Jeanette and Wilbur Pike; one who taught me about the magic of books, the other who taught me about no-nonsense straight-line thinking.

Table of Contents

Acknowledgments	ix
Introduction	xi
One: Two Incompatible Worlds	1
Two: The Asset of Diversity	23
Three: People are the Cause, Tools, and Effect	41
Four: Leading the Discipline of Transition	59
Five: Bridging Two Worlds	71
Six: A Checklist for Leading Transitions	85
Seven: Conclusions	103
Index	109

Acknowledgments

In a book such as this one, countless people contribute to the process of creation and completion. To try to list them all would be futile and probably unsuccessful. To not specifically acknowledge the most profound contributors however would be unconscionable.

First, to Ted Butler and all my friends at Taylor and Fenn, for letting me in on the ground floor.

To Tom Peters whose videos have inspired me to want to know more about transitions and the people who lead them.

To Peter Senge, whose eloquence in describing the power in empowerment has provided great clarity for me.

To Barbara and Richard Monks, in whose cottage in the woods I wrote most of this book.

To Lois Anderson whose eleventh-hour editing and calm kept me out of hot water.

To Cindy Tokumitsu at Quality Resources, for quiet persistence, patience, and professionalism.

Lastly, to Cynthia Shahen and Ann Flesor, for enduring my friendship during the formation of this book and for inspiring me to move forward despite fear and pain.

Thank You.

Introduction

It was threatening to be a very long and tense meeting. As the internal training consultant assigned to assess a work team's readiness for self-management, my job was tricky to say the least. Instead of a meeting with the actual trainees, this meeting was with the human resource generalist, who had sold them on the concept of self-management in the first place. She recently experienced some of our introductory team decision-making training and really felt she knew which of the new problem-solving tools were best suited to this new team. The meeting would be tricky because this HR manager was both an asset and a liability. She was committed to the idea and practice of a new team-empowerment initiative while simultaneously ignoring one of the basic components of the new philosophy, namely, allowing teams to determine and respond to their own needs. Teams that did not need their HR person to decide what was best for them was an idea alien to this manager.

It is probably both unfair and inaccurate to suggest that this HR manager was ill-suited for her job. On the contrary, she was a leader in her company in pushing new ideas into practice throughout her scope of responsibility. As in many large companies, any new initiative to change behavior is often led by the human resources department. It has taken years to finally convince traditional hierarchical managers to rely on their human resource people to lead, or at least contribute to, wide behavioral change within their organizations.

Unfortunately, the primary goal of the team decision-making philosophy is not to change human behavior. It is an attempt to work toward the highest levels of quality on a never-ending upward spiral of improvement. Whereas no improvement is possible without change, the primary motive is quality, not change. If a serious, dyed in the wool quality-team leader could get the maximum quality from a team without having to change the team performance in any way, that would be ideal. Change adds complexity; the goal is to achieve the highest level of performance, not to find things to change. But change in behavior is usually needed to achieve the desired performance. Change must *serve* the business goal.

The team-oriented continuous improvement movement was not started by "people" people. It was started by technical people. The discipline itself is a purely technical model; the human factors are measured, assessed, and controlled. In addition, the concept of self-managed work teams owes its origin to simplicity, not the potential for human development. It simply makes sense to have the people closest to the problem serve as the group to analyze and solve it. The traditional ideas of a management hierarchy approving and leading the process is merely an unnecessary step that slows the process and often adds complex political issues to the team performance, without adding benefit.

The purpose of this book is to help people build bridges between team-centered decision making at the operator level and the traditional management structures. These traditional structures will have to eventually change if the quality movement is to be a lasting contribution to organizational work processes.

The Marriage Contract

This book is really about a marriage. It is about finding leaders who can act as marriage brokers to create a union of different needs. These needs can be met only when a synergistic blend of the assets of both players is achieved. Like all good marriages, this one is a symbol of the understanding that the partners must possess to endure the stresses and trials of living life together. The fundamental differences in gender represented in a typical marriage are no more profound than the differences between the technical and human considerations that must be married to complete a successful transition to a team-oriented, group decision-making operating system.

Too often, the process used by modern companies to change their traditional hierarchic structures and practices to a team-centered, operator-level decision-making system has been based on an unbalanced assumption about what will actually work. The assumption has been that if the technical system in which people work is structured correctly, human considerations and needs will simply be addressed by this system.

Consider the following illustration. For the better part of three years in my private consulting practice, I served as the organizational psychologist for a company that sold statistical process control reengineering services to other companies. Basically, they entered into a company, studied it for two or three weeks to assess the effectiveness of the operating systems, and then made detailed cost-saving recommendations that could improve these systems. In fact, they were so certain of their ability to help companies save money through improved systems and procedures, that they were willing to parlay their fees against the improved outcome. If they didn't save money, they didn't collect their fees.

My job was to serve as the general organizational psychologist and to focus specifically on finding ways to reduce the high turnover rate among the sales force. The typical salesperson in the company had a tenure expectancy of less than one year when I began. The training costs to prepare one salesperson were exorbitant, and the high turnover rate was severely depleting profits.

For a while, I lived and traveled with the CEO and founder of this organization. Because his leadership was so central to the operation of the whole corporation, I needed to be clear on his philosophies and beliefs if I were to serve the company with any degree of integrity and consistency. Aside from studying a delightfully complex person whose life outlook was unique, I also discovered the core cause of the high turnover rate, although I did not recognize it when I saw it.

We were sitting in his flat in London and I told him that one of my other client organizations was making a transition to self-managed work teams to improve performance. He interrupted my story and said, "Teams and human considerations have nothing to do with improving performance. High performance is achieved through control of systems and no other way. This team crap is nothing but hype to keep the masses satisfied that they're important when in fact, once the proper systems are in place, workers will have no other alternative but to perform according to plan."

Now, as I look back, I can see that this belief pervaded his entire organization. The sales-force training, for example, consisted of rote memorization of dialogue for the salesperson to recite, and no deviation was tolerated. Unfortunately, these salespeople worked independently all over the world and the likelihood of finding a person who had the initiative and self-discipline to work alone, as well as tolerate rote memorization of a script to which they had no input, was highly unlikely. High turnover was not only probable, it was virtually ensured.

To ignore or resist the basic nature of those who do the work is folly, yet many companies believe that is what will be achieved by focusing exclusively on the technical aspects of process improvement. The technical disciplines of continuous improvement cannot be minimized. However, these disciplines do not solely make the improvements. It is the people who apply these disciplines that make improvements.

Marriage Survival Components

The content of this book focuses on four primary components that I believe are central to the ability to lead organizations from hierarchic to operator-empowered decision making. The actual number of components is uncertain because some components are subsets of others.

Successfully shifting the power base from the top executives to the people who operate the systems is a remarkably demanding task. My research leads me to believe that the following four issues must be addressed, understood, and operationalized in order to achieve a successful transition:

1. Executive understanding of the philosophy of continuous improvement and operator empowerment. Spending lots of company money does not neces-

sarily indicate understanding. The willingness and ability of executives to embrace the shift of power from the top levels to the lower levels is crucial and should be demonstrated through executive modeling and leadership.

2. Thorough, organization-wide communication is the primary vehicle for every aspect of the transition.

3. The realization that a truly effective transition will be an evolutionary process. This process, which demonstrates the very outcomes it is designed to achieve, will not easily adhere to preset structures, rules or systems. In fact, a true quality philosophy will encourage any solution that accomplishes the desired outcome most effectively. Preset rules for achieving quality are perceived as destructive restrictions.

4. The actual plan and process of the transition should model the desired outcome. Thus, CEOs shouldn't be leading a transition to team-centered decision making, teams should. If the ultimate message is that people will be expected to identify, research, and solve their own operating problems, then the transition system itself should be consistent with that goal.

The remaining chapters will focus on these four components and dissect them in detail, but a full understanding of their fundamental roles in the transitional process will set the stage more effectively.

Executive and Senior Management
Understanding of the New Philosophy

Although this may appear as an obvious requirement, the actual existence of this component among companies attempting a transition is remarkably rare. From an adult-educational point of view, there are few examples of understanding of the profound differences between traditional hierarchic philosophy and philosophies of employee job ownership and decision making. The lack of examples or models makes real understanding much harder to achieve.

I have had a unique opportunity to watch and participate in an attempted transition to a team-oriented, decision-making operating philosophy in my work within the financial services environment. I was working with the corporate training department, and my associates and I were consulting and training newly formed teams to change the way they improved the company's performance. A nationally known training vendor was contracted—without input solicited from the corporate training group—to create a formal series of training programs in TQM problem-solving methodology. A group of human resource executives worked with the vendor to plan a process for a two-year initiative to convert the company. The corporate training group was enlisted to lead the training effort, and the vendor was free to certify others in the company to become trainers as well. For a while, the hot words were "total quality," "self-directed work teams," "continuous improvement," and "six sigma." Our library of videos and articles was backlogged for weeks with requests for materials.

The greatest indicator that the target philosophies were misunderstood was the 30 requests we had in three months to work with departments to "turn them into self-directed work teams." Only a few people involved had any idea of what they were actually seeking or suggesting. After decades of conservative hierarchic tradition, it was unrealistic to believe that the company could switch to a self-directed work style and structure in two years. Our clients repeatedly demonstrated that they thought this change was all about classes, programs, and materials. Virtually no one recognized what a radical departure the new philosophy was from their long-standing identity. In addition, the corporate training consultants were trying to provide good customer service when the customer's request was virtually impossible. Almost as a point of humor my associates and I developed a response to the requests for self-managed work teams, primarily designed to force the requesting manager to see the potential outcome of the request.

Requester: We need you guys to come in here and turn our groups into self-managed work teams and we need it fast.

Ed. Consultant: Are your groups working as teams now?

Requester: Well, no. They're always asking me what to do next or to approve their last bit of work. It's taking all of my time up so I need them to be self-managed, preferably within the next sixty days. Can you handle this, or do I have to use a vendor?

Ed. Cons.: You're free to spend your training development money wherever you wish. For the sake of argument, if we were to successfully comply with your request, have you given any thought as to what you'd like to do for a living once we're done?

Requester: What do you mean?

Ed. Cons.: Well, self-managed means self-managed. Groups that have reached that developmental plane do not need the services of a traditional manager any longer. The role and identity that the previous manager held changes to one of coordinator of team initiatives, facilitator of team interaction, and advocate for the team among other departments.

Requester: That's crazy. Groups always need a manager. Who would assign them their work?

Ed. Cons.: They'll make their own decisions about work assignments. Your job would be to share with them the broad vision of the total company so they can figure out the best way to support that vision by maximizing the resources they have on their team.

Requester: That sounds wonderful in a perfect world, but my people don't have the skills to think and act like that. If I let them do what you just described, we'd get killed by senior management for a lack of control. You're not describing what I'm looking for here at all.

Ed. Cons.: It sounds like we need to talk about your needs in better detail. We can help your groups take more personal initiative and begin to make some team decisions on their own, but the process of converting most groups to true self-management normally takes years. The spectrum of ways for a team to work together is extremely wide and, frankly, no point on that spectrum is innately of higher value than any other. The group's work should be based on the demands of the customer, and that should determine the level of manager involvement within the group. Let's set a time to really look at the results you need within 60 days and see if we can't find a way to get you there.

Requester: OK. I thought this was going to be easy but it doesn't sound like it now.

As preposterous as this dialogue sounds, it does represent several situations in which I and my associates have participated. Although these clients have had solid track records of performance within the traditional operating methods of the financial services business, the problem which isn't about skills or ability, it's about understanding what the transition target represents. That lack of understanding was then effectively modeled to the managers by their bosses.

A Thorough Communication Plan and Implementation

It is inaccurate to isolate this concept as a separate component because it pervades every aspect of organizational success regardless of the driving operational philosophy. When the focus of the communication function is specific to the transition application, then the entire transition plan is only as good as the system in place to make people aware of the new behavioral targets. The plan also provides for operators and leaders to effectively measure and adjust the process once it is implemented.

It is important here to define communication, which can seem like an abstract concept. By "communication" I mean the sharing of all the thoughts, philosophies, transition plans, process evaluations, and team structuring and constituency plans — virtually every facet of the transition attempt.

Generally, the requirements for clear communication will fall into two very different categories: communication about results and output, and communication about the process by which those results and outputs are achieved.

For example, in the chapters on the detailed steps of

leading a successful transition, I advocate that the leader must carefully withhold information about the development of the transition team's internal operations or risk resistance from those in the organization upon whom the intended changes will have the greatest impact. This may seem a contradiction to the fundamental requirement of thorough communication. The contradiction is removed however if one thinks of communication as those messages which relate most realistically to the receiver of the message rather than the sender.

If a team leader is trying to decide what and how to communicate to the organization outside the team, then the goal is to send the messages that mean the most to the people outside the team, or in other words, to communicate about results. The people outside the team want to know "what they're doing on that team" rather than "how" they're doing it; they want to know what the impact of the team's results will have on their current lives.

If the leader makes the mistake of sending messages about the highly dynamic, nonhierarchical, team-based decision making that is a part of the work within the team, and doesn't stress the actual results of that decision making, then people outside the team are threatened, confused and resistant.

So the fundamental requirement of an effective communication plan is a highly demanding one. Issues of what, when, and how to communicate need to be decided by transition leadership *before* the transition begins. The maintenance of the communication plan throughout the transition is perhaps the most vital component to success.

The transition initiative's communication plan is usually the primary responsibility of executive management or the transition leadership. Because the fourth component deals with the modeling requirement for executive leadership, then the communication plan (of which behavior modeling is one form) is the immediate responsibility of the initiators of the power shift. This component will be covered in greater detail throughout this book.

Transition as an Evolutionary Process

Because changing the ownership of decision making should not be led by programmatic or pre-packaged training programs, this component seems to be easily understandable. It simply makes logical behavioral sense that if leaders realize that the transition to team-centered decision making is to remain effective beyond the transition period, then the actual transition process will develop an identity of its own, demonstrating its own evolutionary trends.

When Ralph Stayer, CEO of Johnsonville Foods decided to attempt a total transition from hierarchic to worker-centered decision making, his first attempts failed badly, largely because the transition plan was more or less his, not the result of letting teams plan how to achieve the desired outcomes. Later he realized that his job was to communicate only the broadest based goals and direction, with non-focused direction about the processes he wanted to implement, and that deciding upon the transition implementation details would become one of the first tasks for teams. The pace, content, and process of the transition would increasingly become the responsibility of those who would live with the new philosophy, and that process would evolve over time.

Japanese industrial leaders have turned this idea into a behavioral art form. Peter Senge in *The Fifth Discipline* (Doubleday, 1990) has done a great job at capturing for Americans the idea that the key to effective leadership is never to set autocratic direction, but instead to suggest a general direction that seems to make the best sense for the company. The operators of the company are then allowed to test the supposition that the leaders have suggested and, if it appears sound from an operational perspective, plan a way to achieve that goal. The actual outcomes usually will closely resemble the general idea originally suggested by top leadership. However, the process used to achieve these outcomes will become part of an evolutionary developmental plan owned and operated by the line staff.

The Actual Plan for the Transition Should Model the Desired Outcomes

It is likely that this component is an outcome of the first component, full understanding of the philosophical power shift. Once leaders are fully committed to the new operating philosophy of team decision making and operator control of processes, then the look, feel and behavior of the transition plan will convey that understanding. Ralph Stayer's first attempt was incorrect because it was not a transition team's plan. If the desired outcome is a team decision-making and problem-solving operating system, then the transition itself should be designed to demonstrate that outcome.

This requirement, called "recursiveness" in the training business, often manifests itself in highly creative behaviors from transition sponsors and leaders. I can still see the CEO of a client of mine, who had charged a team with finding a better way to improve customer service, standing in the company cafeteria with the full company gathered. He was dressed in a ringmaster's costume carrying a whip and a large hoop. The sounds of circus music filled the room as he announced that the greatest show on earth was about to get even better. He paraded his team in front of everyone and introduced them one at a time as the group who was about to find ways to jump through this customer service hoop whenever the customer demanded it.

He then handed the whip, hoop, and ringmaster's top hat to the team leader and placed a circus button on each team member. The team leader took over the microphone and told the audience what to expect from each member of the team, each with a specific assignment to accomplish. The laughter and fun in the room was absolutely contagious but the seriousness of the intent was not lost on this audience. Six weeks later the list of improvements was impressive and the total commitment of all employees to achieve those improvements was exceptionally high.

In contrast, one telltale sign of the impending failure of the financial services company's transition discussed earlier became evident to me while the company was at its height in the "new quality" process. Independent of and unrelated to the "quality shift," it was decided by the senior leaders of human resources and key training managers to conduct the first really accurate companywide assessment of the cost of training throughout the corporation. Dubbed "The Training Study," the plan was designed and implemented by some high level executives, and it required hundreds of people to gather data for which none of their data systems were designed. Countless hours of manual data gathering were invested and the political influences from each training manager trying to protect his or her budget made most of the data gathered highly suspect.

The sign which let me know that both the training study and the larger ongoing "new quality" initiative were doomed occurred during a meeting to answer questions about the training study. One of the leading proponents of the new quality-team behaviors asked if the training study would incorporate quality practices to gather the necessary data or to question and challenge the conclusions which the data would generate. I thought it was a great question but I was not surprised at the answer. The key designer of the training study replied in a straightforward tone that the study would not incorporate tenets of the new quality processes because she and other key leaders of the study were not familiar enough with quality tenets and practices, and that the study itself would be used to determine whether the new training for quality was effective or not.

Here was an excellent opportunity to model and demonstrate the team decision making process which, if correctly operated, would have drastically reduced the political contamination of data. In addition, it would create new data gathering processes which could be used by all departments to ensure consistency. The revelation that the senior leaders were untrained in and unfamiliar with the team-process design spelled certain failure for both the study and the larger "new quality" initiative.

Incompatible Families

If we continue with the idea of the transition leader serving as a marriage broker, joining the worlds of the technical and interpersonal, then we can extend the analogy to the larger circle of the marriage of incompatible families. The hierarchic world and the world of team-oriented decision making have very little in common in the way that work lives are led. The expectation for effective leaders who will facilitate the top-to-bottom power shift is uniquely demanding.

Because most of the companies I have studied and worked with have no intention of totally abandoning their hierarchic structure, at least at the beginning of the transition period, we present the transition team with the unenviable task of learning to live in two worlds simultaneously, with each world recognizing totally different reward and behavior structures. The requirement is similar to asking a bride and groom to fit in with each other's families without disruption when those two families are different in history, religion, culture, traditions, language, and expectations. Only, in the case of transition team members, the two worlds are demanding different behaviors at exactly the same moment. This book is an attempt to help leaders realize these fundamental requirements and discover ways to lead the transition such that the desired outcome is permanent and enduring. The intention here is to focus on the details of successfully balancing the technical with the human considerations and more broadly, on the balance between the traditional hierarchical expectations and the newer team-centered decision making.

A Note About Language

It is virtually impossible to discuss the issues in this book without the use of labels. The labels used to describe philosophies like Total Quality Management, Continuous Improvement, Empowerment, and Process Reengineering all serve to focus attention on a new and different thought process. At the same time, those labels represent a serious restriction to thought and potential.

In the last several years of his life, W. Edwards Deming would not use the words "quality" or "continuous improvement" in any of his work. He was intensely aware of the damage done by those who had reduced the movement to a series of practices, steps, or tools used as bandages for their injured companies.

The evolutionary component discussed earlier illustrates that the labels used to describe the transition process relate only to our own experiences.

When I tell people about my research, it is not uncommon for them to say, "Oh, we tried TQM in our shop and it didn't work." The restriction implied in that reaction is an important obstacle to overcome in the transition. I strive here to minimize the TQM label's stereotyping by utilizing a variety of terms and descriptions to capture the essence of team structures and worker-level decision making (itself a label), and not focusing on specific labels.

I instead concentrate on understanding the philosophies they name.

Another frequently used term may cause some confusion without clarification. The word *leader* has several connotations that can be restrictive. I broadly refer to leadership as behaviors that are designed to influence others who share common goals. Leadership is a behavioral construct, whereas management is a positional construct. It is possible that the CEO who sponsors a transition to a better way of decision making within his or her organization is a leader, but the label is not guaranteed by virtue of his or her position. The title of leader is earned on the basis of how that CEO performs in the transition process.

In addition, the hourly employee placed on a transition team may become a strong leader without any hierarchical rank. One of the most exciting possibilities of empowerment is the potential for people to grow personally, and the team structure encourages the development of natural leadership in its members. People follow leaders because they believe that their own interests will be served and because they believe in the leader's behavioral model. The most liberal concept of a leader will serve more effectively here than one with narrow parameters.

ONE

Two Incompatible Worlds

American organizations attempting to move to new philosophies of decision making from a traditional hierarchy have success rates that are sporadic at best. The SPC/TQM process wizards have analyzed the reasons for the difficulty of the transitions with all the highly focused tools and techniques of their trade. The explanations for the failures range from inadequate training to not enough test time to the big favorite, lack of senior executive buy-in to the new philosophies. None of these reasons really captures why American organizations aren't very good at adopting practices in which decision making is the responsibility of employees and not managers. The track record for transitions resulting in permanent changes to the way organizations do business is not good.

The problem isn't about using the right tools or building the right teams, or allowing enough time for teams to learn the new approaches. And although total senior executive buy-in does overcome a lot of obstacles, some companies have been able to achieve some successes without it. Indeed, these behaviors are serious obstacles to successful employee-centered performance; however, they are only symptoms of the real problem.

The real problem in making the transition to employee-centered performance is that we do not adequately deal with the reality of living in one world with all it's language, culture, and assumptions, while simultaneously learning to live in a new world with completely different language, culture, and assumptions. The real problem is all about learning profoundly different ways to survive while using old survival skills to stay alive while you learn.

Imagine the outcomes of governmental structure in the U.S. if our democratic philosophies were developed and gradually put into practice while a king still maintained ultimate control. In fact, such a demand upon the "workers" would cause a war in which the "workers" redesigned the rules of battle out of sheer desperation. They simply could not continue to function with one foot in each camp.

Or picture a wagon master in the early 1800s as he prepares settlers for the trip across the new frontier. His charges are motivated to go and think they are ready to begin the adventure. He knows that he alone cannot prepare the settlers with all that they'll need to survive. He knows that the real key lies within them as a group. If they will pull together and communicate, tell the truth to each other, and agree to solve problems fully from their own resources then their chances of success are increased, although still not guaranteed. The settlers want the wagon master to tell them the rules of survival so they will be able to adapt. Because, in the highly "civilized" world of which they are products, that is what survival is all about — find out the rules and comply. However, he cannot teach them what they'll need to survive. The answers are inside them.

He does know that his role is most vital as the trip begins because the new patterns of behavior must be set carefully. Once set, the trip itself will be the best teacher.

The Obstacle of Success

Perhaps the Japanese got a head start in the modern race to achieve business success because they were defeated in World War II. Their industry and economy were in disarray after the war, and old habits, ways of doing business, even attitudes about the nature of work were all thought to have contributed to defeat. At an AMA Human Resources Conference in 1993, Peter Senge quoted W. Edwards Deming, who when asked why the Japanese took his messages to heart replied, "You have to understand. They had nothing." In fact, with the principles of Deming and others, the potential to start from scratch can be seen today as a significant advantage over the manufacturing practices and post-war prosperity of the United States. Nothing demonstrates this fundamental refusal of the United States to look at a different way of thinking as does the rejection of Deming's ideas here before he went to Japan. We knew how to make things correctly, quickly, and inexpensively after the war, and the leaders of American industry were eager to get to the big profits of post war consumerism. Not only were the concepts of SPC and TQM alien to the American way of doing business, there seemed to be absolutely no reason on the immediate or long-range horizon to even consider them.

The same military models which spelled defeat to the Japanese spelled success to American business. The history of industries like manufacturing, construction, or insurance all show a huge post-war boom accompanied by drastic organizational adjustments to respond to growth. The people who were charged with responding to these challenges were often recent ex-military managers. It isn't hard to find companies today in which people still are closely tied to strong delineations of rank and level.

Real and Distinct Differences

Recently, while delivering a course in project management to a group of inexperienced project managers, a clear example of the fundamental problem of transition was presented. I was illustrating the changes the company was undergoing by asking participants to share how the assumptions about their work had changed over the last two years. The answers consisted of powerful examples ranging from tremendously expanded span of control, to complex matrix project approaches, to total chaos, when two of the participants offered a perfect example.

"I'm Bill Jones," said one, "and I am the project manager on a huge new project which will ultimately change the entire process by which my department does its work."

"This is Dan Clusler," continued Bill, "a specialist in systems redesign and unofficially the second in command on the team. His knowledge is absolutely vital to the success of the project. Dan is my boss when we're not working on this project. He selected me to lead the team and I selected him to head the systems subgroup on the project. We work constantly to avoid confusion about roles and if we weren't already good friends before I came to work here, we would have no chance at maintaining effective work relationships either on or off the project. In fact, it is touch and go as it is."

As we continued to explore this leadership juxtaposition with the class, it was agreed that no one else in the class thought that they could maintain such a confusing set of reporting relationships for very long. The project was set to last for 18 months, and except for rare cases like Bill and Dan's whose personal relationship was strong and independent of work, the group felt such a situation was simply not workable.

As I continued to probe their thinking it became evident that the most insurmountable problems related to social and interpersonal skills, formal evaluation of performance, and confusion to other subordinates about who was who. The problem wasn't about tools or processes or philosophies, it was about maintaining personal identity when those identities kept shifting.

The class agreed that the fluid reporting relationships, which shifted depending on which work was being done, were not effective unless those involved had strong enough interpersonal relationships to carry them above the positional roles of management. Those relationships were largely absent at work, with Dan and Bill being the exception rather than the rule. The class also agreed that the company was making no real effort to help people develop the necessary interpersonal skills. The impact of those facts on the requirements for effective transitions to team-based decision making creates serious problems for transition leaders and may indicate a lack of awareness of the required interpersonal skills.

Dan and Bill's project ended up successfully, and when I had the chance to talk to Bill, the project manager, he explained that the way he and Dan avoided the barriers of flip-flopping management roles was to constantly talk about those roles and recognize that they could function effectively in either the follower or leader role, regardless of assigned position. In fact, what finally worked for them was to remain totally focused on the goals and results of the project rather than who was "in charge."

Already noted in this work is the difficulty of defining transition labels. A subset of the difficulty is the problem of defining roles and situations of people who come to join the transition process. Here are some of the more significant role descriptions:

Sponsor

Sponsors actually initiates a transition. Usually they are high enough in the hierarchy to fund, staff and direct the outcome of the transition. They are not members of the transition team, although they often work closely with the team to ensure adequate communication. The hierarchic level of the sponsor usually indicates the size and seriousness of the transition goals. For example, at Johnsonville Foods, the intent of the transition was a total redefining of the way work gets done and of who will make the decisions within the work process. That kind of a transition would need the sponsorship of the person at the top of the organization and, in fact, Ralph Stayer was CEO when the idea began.

On the other hand, if the transition is to find a new way to deal with and reduce the cost of alternate mail services in one small department, for example, then the department manager would appoint a team leader to suggest improvements to the current process. In the case of the insurance company discussed earlier, as the team began to gather data and suggest new ways to send mail, the project began to attract interest from other larger mail users. Each time new departments were added to the project, the sponsor changed and the level of each succeeding sponsor moved upward so that the final sponsor of the project at completion was the chief operating officer of the division.

Transition Team

The transition team is charged with achieving the goals of the intended transition. Usually they represent a cross-section of the resources needed to complete the transition, both from the current operation view and the projected outcome view. The use of "team members" refers to those people who have been removed from the "line organization" where the work is routinely done and placed on a team designed to study and revise the way that work will be done in the future. Traditionally, the line organization continues to do the work in the established manner while the team studies the opportunities to improve the process.

Team construction, content, and groundrules can be a highly changeable process as the objectives of the team become clearer. Depending on the stage of work the team is involved in, the size and diversity of the team can vary drastically. The effectiveness of the changes within the team is usually an indication of the skills of the team leader and the relationship between that leader and the project sponsor.

When an associate of mine was the leader of a team created to design the next generation of management training classes, she gathered the sponsor and several key line managers together to set realistic behavioral goals for the next generation of managers. This was a very controversial discussion, and the more they talked the more they added other "experts" to their discussions. Once they hammered out several basic goals for this training curriculum, she thanked these leaders and dismissed the group. Then she built a whole new team containing more training experts than business leaders, although several line managers who served on her first team served here as advisors. The actual training design was accomplished by this second team. Once they had created a set of course outlines and approaches, the leader created a third team to field test the classroom experience.

Each of those teams had different goals and required a different approach from the leader. Some people served on all three teams, yet their roles and expectations changed with each new focus.

In the following paragraphs, we will explore what each of two contrasting systems — the two worlds — requires of its workers and look in detail at how those requirements differ. We will see that the differences aren't only about the way we do business, they're about what people need emotionally to feel secure, stable, and effective.

The Hierarchical World

In examining this world, we will focus on the areas that enable people to survive and thrive within the hierarchy.

The fundamental tenets of hierarchical organizations in the U.S. are based on several assumptions that were far more realistic in the post-war U.S. than they are now. The view of the human resources component, especially, may be based on outmoded assumptions.

Hierarchy works best when:

1. There is a stable, endless labor force. (There'll always be enough people who need jobs.)

2. Entry into the organization is accompanied by a lack of information about organizations, product knowledge or specific job expertise. (However, new hires can acquire skills through training that will meet specific needs.)

3. The market place is small enough that most of the key players know each other and there is tacit, unspoken agreement on the rules of competition. (We know all the players in our network as well as their respective strengths and weaknesses, which remain largely constant. If they change, we'll react.)

4. Results and rewards within the organization are

based on compliance and extrinsic rewards are adequately satisfying to their recipients. (People will be happy if you pay them enough. What they do and how they do it isn't for them to decide. Few of us would be here if it wasn't for the money.)

The world in which these assumptions were true has changed. The nature of work, as well as the size, education level, and expectations of the workforce has changed. The competitive playing field is now worldwide and the approaches far too complex for reactive decision making to assure survival. Yet the majority of U.S. organizations still cling to these ideas simply because they have made such great sense for so long. The popularity of TQM and new reengineering concepts shows recognition of the need to change, but the resistance to behavioral change is very powerful and often an unconscious reaction.

Recently, a manager who is well respected in her organization said, "We really do need to learn these TQM tools because once the market place calms down and we can afford to get back up to full staffing levels, we're going to need better tools to keep control of our efficiency."

The world will likely become an increasingly difficult place for this type of manager. Fears about losing control of the system will appear to be coming true and worst of all, the employees may blame it all on this manager.

The World of Team-Centered, Operator-Level Decision Making

Deming stopped using the words "Quality," "TQM," or "Continuous Improvement" in his presentations and was adamant about the idea that this movement isn't about labels. Once we label something, it appears to have a clear identity. In addition, we assume, that things with the same label are identical. When a manager says "we tried that TQM stuff and it didn't work," it is pretty certain that he has applied his own interpretation to TQM philosophy, and we have no real idea what he really means.

What we call or name the process isn't very important. More important is that the process which that ownership of responsibility operates will not be the same from organization to organization or even the same within one organization. That is, if the ultimate goal is maximized performance as defined by the actual performance group, then the process by which it is achieved will differ from group to group, even within the same organization.

Broadly defined, TQM, reengineering, and similar practices mean, "The series of decisions and other behaviors which result from a philosophy in which:

- Each member of the organization take personal responsibility for his/her job output.

- Each work group take responsibility for the quality of their collective input, including the analysis and resolution of problems that affect their work processes.

- All work is viewed as part of a process that can be altered to improve quality.

- The manager's job consists of facilitating effective group and individual development, coaching the development of individuals and groups, and providing groups with resources with which to improve performance.

- All systems, structures, and processes within an organization are designed to enable people to work more effectively and can therefore be questioned, altered, eliminated or increased to serve higher performance."

As with hierarchy, there are several primary assumptions upon which this definition is based. These assumptions represent the fundamental beliefs which must be accepted to make the definition operational:

1. People can and will take personal ownership of the outcomes of their jobs. (People want their work to matter.)

2. People who are closest to the problems at work are the best candidates to solve them.

3. People will generate effective ideas to improve performance once they are clear on the expectations for performance. (People need to know the goals and objectives in order to make sound decisions.)

4. Managers who view their role as police and behave consistent with that view do not serve the developmental needs of the group and therefore deteriorate the group potential. (People need coaches, not cops.)

The attractiveness and simplicity of this approach are two of the leading motivators for senior executives to consider shifting to TQM/reengineering in the first place.

It is only when we place the respective approaches of hierarchy next to those of TQM (or whatever label the reader prefers) that the reason for the repeated failures in the transitions becomes clear. The problem is that the rules and structures of each approach are behaviorally incompatible, especially when operated simultaneously.

The following chart offers short descriptions of functions that affect people within the operation of any organization. Although there are exceptions to the statements shown, they represent general descriptions of survival facts for hierarchies and TQM environments.

FUNCTION	SURVIVAL INFORMATION	
	HIERARCHY	TQM
GOALS		
Setting	Done at the top of the organization. May be based on solicited information from lower ranks.	Done by work group related to current initiative. Coordinated with other work teams.
Communicating	From top down through management chain.	From each work group throughout the organization.
Implementing	At operator level based on supervisor direction.	By work group—self-directed.
Measuring	At middle and top managerial levels. May not happen at all	By work group. Used to redesign goals.
ASSUMPTIONS ABOUT PEOPLE		
Compliance/ Commitment	People will comply with management directives.	People will commit to stringent goals of their own design
Measurement/ Evaluation	People should be evaluated on performance and attitude (initiative).	People will design and conduct their own evaluation system
Decision-Making	People need specialized training or experience to make correct work decisions.	People will make sound decisions based on the information they have available.
	People can be expected to follow instructions and behave consistently without individual decision-making.	People will make sound decisions balanced between the needs of individual and the needs of the group.
Growth and Development	Responsibility for individual growth and development is loosely assigned to the manager. Growth is usually closely related to and discussed in context with the requirements of the current job.	Responsibility for individual growth belongs primarily to the individual. Growth paths are related to current and future needs of the work team.

FUNCTION	SURVIVAL INFORMATION	
	HIERARCHY	**TQM**

DECISION MAKING

Managerial	Determined by the number of people or dollars involved—the larger the impact the farther up the decision should be made.	Managers do not decide issues for work teams. Managers decide how to best support work team initiatives.
Process	Gather information from people with the problem or need, consult others, manager decides.	Team process, based on team goals or problems. Team consensus is the operational norm.
Measurement	Generally through observation of implemented managerial solution. Often measured by whether or not the problem goes away.	Conducted by team against previously set standards.

ROLES OF GROUPS AND TEAMS

Formation	Teams may be formed for temporary projects. Groups who work together in a department often are called teams without any change in group identity, practices or membership.	Teams are formed to solve problems or improve work. Teams are self-managed and set ground rules for operation. Once established teams are completely self-sufficient.
Autonomy and Authority	Usually related to the position of the group manager or team sponsor. Seldom identified specifically or assigned to the team or group.	Work teams have sponsors who delegate authority and autonomy to meet group goals.
Structures	Teams which are officially acknowledged usually have assigned leadership. Rules, policies, modeled behavior flow from the assigned leader to the team members.	All work team structure, policies, norms, rules are determined and enforced by team members only. All team structures are designed to achieve team objectives and may change as objectives change.

The human interactive requirements are both the problem and the solution to living successfully in incompatible worlds, and leaders who are clear on those requirements are the only ones who will be successful in making the change.

Commitment Doesn't Mean Understanding

Much of the current literature addressing the failure of TQM and reengineering initiatives arrives at a few similar conclusions. Certainly near the top of that list of reasons for the failure is "lack of senior management commitment." Although there are countless stories of executives who set in motion the concept of transition and then did not provide the resources to make it happen, that is not the usual scenario. A competent hierarchical manager would easily recognize the folly of such a behavior and seek to avoid it. The real failure at the senior level isn't from a lack of commitment. It is much more fundamental than that. Executive failure occurs because executives don't really understand the profound impact of letting employees have control over their own work. Too often, executives think that this power shift will be a temporary solution to poor traditional performance and once things are happily profitable again, the organization will return to life as it was. The flaw in that logic is clear for people who really do understand the fundamental differences between the empowered and hierarchical philosophies.

Many transition attempts might have been handled differently, or perhaps not at all, if someone whom the CEO trusted told him or her:

> This new process will alter the very essence of everything this organization says and does permanently regardless

of the impact on profits or success. Once you are past a certain point in this transition process you cannot return to the place you are now. Your role as the 'giver and enabler of all action' within the organization will end forever, replaced with a new role of teacher, guide and coach.

When I see what companies have spent in money and human resources to switch to a matrix philosophy while increasing hierarchical boundaries and structures to facilitate the switch, I am more and more convinced that they simply don't understand what the new philosophy really means. Often the transition is structured with restrictive boundaries and multi-level sign-offs to make sure the status quo is not threatened.

One indicator that key executives do not really understand the implications in their acceptance of the transition philosophy may be found in the practice of rushing to a large, standardized approach, usually led by an external vendor. Successful leaders of effective power shifts will tell you that the actual transition process is a product of the whole concept. It is evolutionary, taking on the idiosyncracies of the people, environment, and marketplace of the parent organization. There is no set formula to reach the destination, no clear time frame for arrival, no guarantee that the process won't have lots of starts and stops, as well as small successes and failures.

This does not mean that the use of an external vendor is unwise or unnecessary. It means that the timing and parameters of the use of vendors is often an intuitive process. Once the organization's members have developed real clarity with the transition sponsors about the actual intended outcomes, they can feel both the right time and the extent to which they should involve vendors. If the process is properly set, the transition participants experience the full value of the vendor without defensiveness or confusion.

In the Introduction, I offered the example of an associate who was charged with creating the next generation of management training courses for a large corporation. The original sponsor of the project made a strong recommendation early on that the leader use the services of a specific vendor who had created a wonderful new way to deliver classroom training. The sponsor wanted the vendor to be a part of the process from the start and it took some strong communication skills on the part of the leader to get the sponsor to agree to wait before inviting the vendor in. Her argument was that the actual goals of the new curriculum were not clearly set yet and the process to set them should not include an outside vendor with limited knowledge of the challenges that the business lines faced throughout the company. Once the goals and objectives of the entire curriculum were well defined, the leader then invited the vendor to sit as a member of the transition team. The vendor's contribution was highly focused and effective, and the partnership between the vendor and the training designers was based on a common goal without the turf wars which traditionally arise when inside and outside trainers work together.

Comparative Examples:
Financial Services Corporation and Johnsonville Foods

Financial Services Corporation

This example refers to a large financial services corporation that is a major player in that industry. To allow for the most accurate portrayal of this organization's experiences with an unsuccessful TQM transition, it will be left unnamed throughout the book.

The quality transition experience at the financial services corporation reveals some mistakes that are fairly common but hard to see or anticipate. The initial motivation to institute a team-oriented transition came from senior managers who wanted to see if these practices were applicable within a large financial services corporation because most of the models had originated in the manufacturing environment. They wanted to know if these practices could improve profits and general organizational effectiveness. A quality committee was created to look into the idea, and that group began to develop a real sense of excitement about the potential. This sequence of events did not indicate that something was missing, however. That "something" was pivotal to success: executive management never completely understood or experienced the full impact of the target philosophy. They did not realize that they had set in motion a new idea that actually questioned every primary assumption they had used for years to run a large financial services corporation. They did not foresee that the success of the effort would change their own roles and the nature of their organizational control. For them, this initiative was merely a series of training events that might make teams form easier and solve problems more effectively.

Another problem arose when the quality committee began to compare vendors for eventual selection as the catalysts for corporate-wide change. They began to talk to the big national players in TQM transitions. The size of that potential contract would have been seen as intensely attractive by any serious vendor. In hindsight, I think it is likely that the vendors did not have a clear view of how complex the business structures of the corporation really were or how fiercely protective the leaders of the business areas were. In fact, the corporation was, in a sense, composed of five or six separate independent companies. The reason the vendors may not have understood this was because the initiative was conceived above those lines and had a clear corporate stamp on it. The original charge came from the corporate top alone.

Thus, the desired outcomes of the initiative were not clear to the different business lines. From the start, the autonomy of the various business lines was problematic. In addition, none of the professional training departments housed within the business lines were solicited for input until well after the initiative was underway and the vendor in place. The result was a lack of commitment at best and open hostility at worst among the people in the company who knew the most about using training efforts to lead change.

Almost immediately the word *quality* became a corporate buzzword and managers climbed onto the quality bandwagon. The way they demonstrated their commitment was to get their staffs trained in the new "program." The program mentality swept through the company. The corporate management training group was designated as the transitional target group to deliver the training as the vendor gradually faded out of the picture, although that group had not been substantially involved in the initial discussions or the vendor selection. They were chosen for this role because they were large enough to handle it and had a smooth-running administrative system to handle the logistics, such as training room reservations, enrollments, and post-training evaluation.

Literally dozens of sessions of the basic course in group problem solving were delivered. Managers did not always comply with the requirement that intact teams go through the training together, probably because team format was not truly operative or predominant throughout the company. Instead, traditional hierarchy remained deeply embedded. The classes had highs and lows. They ranged from confusing arguments about "what will work in my section" to motivating sessions for intact teams that were ready for this profoundly different step. For most, however, the post-class experience was a return to life as it was before, only now using the tools that the class featured. Some of the more focused teams were actually able to complete important projects with very positive results, but for the majority the whole thing just eventually blew over without too much impact on individuals or their work.

To summarize, this financial services company initiated a TQM transition with the best of intentions. But lack of executive *understanding* of the scope and depth of the change—what many people mistake as lack of executive *commitment*—caused the effort to stumble out of the starting gate in the wrong direction. That, in turn, led to the second serious problem: failure to call upon the skills and goodwill of the very people whose buy-in could pave the way for success, the people who would be most impacted and should be most involved—the business line training departments. Instead, an external vendor was chosen without any input from the business lines.

Johnsonville Foods

The incredible history of Ralph Stayer and Johnsonville Foods is a contrast to the approach at the financial services corporation. Here is a transition that started from the top and hasn't stopped yet. Although Johnsonville Foods was well respected and safely profitable, Ralph Stayer, its CEO, was dissatisfied with the company's failure to adequately return its investment to its employees. Ralph was deeply concerned that his people were unmotivated and uninterested in personal growth at work. He said "if I've done anything right in this whole process, it was to realize that the fault was mine, not theirs." Management blasphemy by most standards of the times, but a place to start for Stayer.

Like most successful TQM stories, the company didn't set out to have a "TQM transition." It became an inevitable outcome because the goal was simply to get people more involved in their work and take more personal ownership of their jobs and outcomes. Teams were formed not for the sake of forming teams, but because Ralph Stayer believed that the best method to improve the way the company did business was to let those doing the work have as much control as possible over their own environment. He did not seek a preset formula to shift his operation, he developed his own formula through the gradually increasing involvement of his people.

The transition process took nearly 10 years before the philosophy was established enough to run itself. There were repeated failures, especially at the beginning. As the philosophy began to develop, Stayer told his employees that he expected them to grow, to set challenging goals, and to try to beat their best performance every day. Many of those employees thought he was crazy, that he was experiencing some serious emotional disorder. Few Johnsonville Foods employees understood or agreed when he announced "it is immoral for a leader of a company or organization not to encourage and allow people to grow to their fullest." But the early failures only led Stayer to review the process of the transition attempt, not the fundamental values. He relied more on the voice of the employee to dictate the best way to get the job done. Stayer managed the shift by clarifying direction and outcomes and deferring to employees to design the best way to get there. Gradually the philosophy began to drive every function of the company. Teams do their own hiring, evaluations, wage increases, firing, training, budgeting, job-area design, and conflict resolution—virtually all decisions that affect the people. The work of the teams and the products they produce have become the responsibility of the teams.

Traditional managers were either eliminated or converted to team coordinators and teachers. They learned never to second guess the decisions of the team, to allow teams to learn through constant clarification of goals and objectives, and to support all decision making with factual analysis.

Although there are skeptics who think this sounds like a nightmare of "soft" management, the teams can and do make very difficult decisions courageously. They decided, for example, that the traditional idea of pay raises was contrary to the personal-growth philosophy. They eliminated all automatic increases and replaced them with team performance bonuses and individual increases based entirely on learning new skills. Employees started at relatively low wages and got increases when they learned how to do budgeting, train the team in a new process, or any other new skill that the team thought added value to their ability to meet goals.

Volumes have been written about the phenomenal transition at Johnsonville Foods and there is no need to repeat it all here. The process has had its ups and downs, and the organization has struggled through problems like any other company. But the one single fact that remains, despite the cyclical successes and failures, is that the philosophy of empowering people to solve their own work-related problems in a highly effective, ethical way still prevails at Johnsonville Foods.

These two cases, the financial services corporation and Johnsonville Foods, illustrate that, at the most fundamental levels, the essence of the successful transition is faith in people. When the financial services corporation as an entity feels any serious threat to its market share, it seeks to pull control away from its operator level people back to the control of a small group of people at the top. However, when Johnsonville feels threatened, Stayer will ask his labor force what they'd like to do about it. The difference is perhaps as profound as we are capable of understanding.

TWO

The Asset of Diversity

This chapter will look, in detail, at the "people" aspect of these transitions, addressing issues of workforce diversity and communication. Despite all the technic advancements that the empowerment or TQM movement has produced, the pulse of the movement is ultimately about people — how they feel, work together, and think.

The people who work in America today are substantially different in many ways from the people who worked in post-war America. During that era the hierarchic structure of American companies developed rigid strength to support their rapid growth. Previously, the age of automation bred the concept that workers can be treated as extensions of the machines they operated, and the war served to reinforce the idea that who makes the products is less important than how they are made. Even though the workforce became more diverse during the war due to the scarcity of adult men, the differences within that workforce were intentionally ignored to facilitate getting the products out the door. In fact, the automated processes developed before and during the war proved that the nature of the worker was unimportant as long as procedures were followed correctly.

The idea that people will come to work who are different from the majority of the workforce is certainly not new to management in America. In fact the concept of the America melting pot was born out of the rapid growth of the American manufacturing movement and the immigration that fed it from the turn of this century through the forties. Because the problems associated with a highly culturally diverse workforce were potentially disruptive to growing organizations during World War II, management throughout the country developed a series of procedures and policies to ensure that new ethnicities and cultures joining the workforce would be quickly mainstreamed into the total workforce population.

After World War II, when the mechanized efficiency movement began new development, the practice of ignoring the demographic differences of the labor force was defined as assimilation. Because the goal was to produce products with absolute sameness (and high quality), it was easy to believe that the workers should sound, look, and act the same. Differences of language, ethnicity, religion, and culture were considered obstacles to assimilation, and the general expectation among business leaders was that individuals would have to find a way to fit in as quickly as possible.

Lest we characterize the assimilation movement as an evil, profit-centered motive of American management, it is important to note that a primary purpose of assimilation was to protect workers from discrimination on the basis of ethnicity or religion. It is not surprising that these attempts to protect workers were supported by a series of federal laws and guidelines.

One reason that confusion and uncertainly still surround the true motives and intent of the assimilation philosophy may be because the structures and assumptions that evolved during the past 50 years in U.S. businesses presume a stable, apparently unlimited labor force. That labor force has changed and continues to change. The rate of change in the demographic mix in the workforce is increasing, too. Those changes have become problematic in many organizations because the rigidity of their systems often makes flexibility a confusing and expensive response.

The assumption that unlimited labor is constantly available is now moot because many organizations have been forced to reduce the size of their labor force. In fact, the size of the available labor force has increased overall but the nature of the changes in work processes require much more careful selection. Because of higher levels of technical proficiency needed to work in the U.S. today, the old assumption that people can start at entry-level positions and "grow" into higher-level positions is, in many industries, defunct. Technology-skilled employees are not in unlimited supply and the cost to create a technology-skilled employee through developmental educational programs is in many places simply too expensive.

One outcome of the search for technically proficient employees is found in the increase of Asian, Indonesian, and Indian populations in the U.S. workforce. But the influx of this population into U.S. organizations often highlights the problems with personnel practices that are still vested in the old philosophies of assimilation. The cultural identities of the new demographic expansion groups are very strong, and often cultural differences are expressed at work. The result is problematic on several levels. First, the potential conflict among the labor force itself is increased. Many American workers have not had the necessary exposure to or training in multi-cultural sensitivity.

I have heard countless employees who come to my workshops on cultural diversity complain that their own ethnicity or national origin was not championed with such programs when they joined the workforce 20 years ago. This already assimilated group insists that all this sensitivity to the differences among new members in the work force will only heighten potential conflicts among ethnic groups. Fortunately, well constructed training programs teach sensitivity to all cultures, including those populations well established here for centuries. The track record among companies that have tried to address diversity issues through training and awareness programs is good at minimizing conflict potential, at least from my own experience as a training consultant, but not all companies are willing to commit the resources for such programs.

Personnel policies that have not kept pace with the rapid changes in the multicultural workforce is another problem area. Too often, the motivation to create effective personnel policies has been the avoidance of conflict rather than ensuring the rights of individuals at work. Policies that clearly list restrictions on behavior instead of positively presenting the goal of individual rights protection are simply inadequate to cover multicultural behaviors that are now present in U.S. organizations. As the trend to revise policies primarily to prevent lawsuits continues, the costs to organizations is substantial and still leaves companies working in reactive rather than proactive modes.

For those organizations that seek a transition to a team-oriented decision-making philosophy, the increasingly complexity of our workforce should be seen as an asset. For those organizations in which the power shift relates only to a series of tools used to maintain hierarchic control, workforce diversity is an obstacle to be controlled and overcome. At the most basic of levels, the company's response to workforce diversity becomes either an asset or a liability, and organizational leaders make a clear choice when they respond.

Diversity and Hierarchy

Responding effectively and sensitively to changes in the workforce requires modern managers to think about workers in a new way. Even if the motivation is present to review and revise our policies relating to diversity, history sometimes interferes. The on again, off again history of assimilation attempts has resulted in confusion and fear among managers about what is and what is not a reasonable approach.

To address this problem, I created a workshop called Effective Performance Discussions. Because this workshop is a specialized communications program, the primary activity in the class consists of a series of increasingly complex role plays that capture some of the powerful work-related interpersonal issues that can only be resolved through one-on-one communication. As each new scenario is revealed to the participants, new models and techniques are offered to resolve the issues. One of the more difficult role plays relates to an employee whose boss feels she isn't assertive enough to get her project leader assignment done on time.

For the employee, the idea of following up on others to see that they meet their respective deadlines without the hierarchic position to do so is culturally aberrant. Indeed, her desire to remain consistent to the identity of her ethnic origin is so strong, it actually becomes a model of assertiveness. Naturally, the role for the supervisor is to confront the employee with the missed deadlines and to discuss what approaches they might take jointly to prevent further problems. It has become a regular occurrence in this program, during this role play, for supervisors to avoid cultural topics at all costs. The employee is ready to discuss her cultural identity and even to resign if the boss insists on violation of it. Yet managers will not initiate the discussion.

When questioned about their avoidance rationale, their responses will range from discomfort with the topic generally to "it's against the law to discuss ethnic or cultural issues with non-American employees." I am always amazed at the absolute certainty with which this last statement is made. When I ask how or why they know it to be true (which it clearly is not), they cannot tell me but they usually will insist on this "fact" just the same.

If managers and supervisors are convinced that cultural and ethnic issues are illegal to discuss, then the development of sensitive approaches and techniques to deal with many of the significant work issues will be stifled.

Here is another example of the managers' mind-set to avoid issues of diversity. I was working on basic communication skills program with a group of supervisors. They were loudly lamenting a repeated behavioral pattern of their Portuguese employees. They said these employees often acknowledged instructions from their supervisors, but their subsequent behavior indicated that they hadn't understood at all.

This was apparently very frustrating to the supervisors, who were confident in their ability to send clear messages. Communication wasn't the problem, they felt, it was the ridiculous habit of their employees of insisting that they understood when they really didn't. The resolution to this problem surprised everyone both in its simplicity and its source. One of the supervisors, a Portuguese-American who was fluent in both languages, said quietly and assuredly: "It's because you all ask the wrong question. The Portuguese people are taught never to challenge their bosses. When you guys give instructions, you always follow them by asking 'do you understand?' For a respectful Portuguese employee, to say no to that question is to insult your boss by suggesting that he hasn't been clear. The employee would rather risk having you think he was stupid than he would potentially insulting you."

I have always used that story to illustrate the importance of drawing feedback from the receiver to instructions, but it also illustrates that managers have not been taught to think in terms of the cultural diversity within their workforce and do not approach those differences as arenas for increased effectiveness. If we were, for example, to simply remove the hierarchic differences between the supervisor and the employee in the previous example (as we would in an empowered work team), the employee might respond in a far more useful way to the question "do you understand?".

Resolutions Are Possible

To resolve the dysfunctionality that results from the fear of diversity in so many companies in the U.S., one must start at the most basic levels. The people actually doing the work, dealing closely with one another, have a much easier time with diversity issues than do their managers. They tend to be less intimidated because they routinely resolve differences to keep their work flowing. If they are free to resolve differences and solve problems at their own level — in a way that gets the job done and remains respectful of all players — then the quality of their response tends to be high and long lasting. This philosophy of letting the people with the problem decide, design, and deliver their own solution is the essence of the TQM approach. In many ways, it has been in place in most companies for many years and now can be elevated to do more than just simply keep the peace.

There is a foundry in Windsor, Connecticut that illustrates the essence of this approach to management. The leadership and philosophies operating this foundry are some of the most progressive I have worked with in the past 15 years. Depending on their work volume and backlog, the ethnic diversity of their workforce can be rather complex.

At the core of this diversity is a strong Portuguese population. As much as 70% of the workforce is Portuguese and many people do not speak English at all or do so only marginally. No effort is made here to ignore the ethnic integrity of the Portuguese people. In fact, it is often championed. The Portuguese are proud to mention that they have been the world's foundrymen since the beginning of foundry technology.

Throughout the foundry work areas, when problems arise about language or culture, the people with the problem are expected to resolve it, respectfully, and sensitively, in their own way. It was the hourly workforce who requested that the company formally designate several people as translators. They produced the list of candidates and arranged for the translators to meet and agree on translation philosophy and interpretation. Now, any employee who speaks either English or Portuguese *must* use only the acknowledged translators when they have an important question about work. This system seldom needs policing, but when it does, it is monitored by hourly employees, not management, because they are its architects and can make the best judgements about its use.

This example is only one small sample of the power of letting people solve their own diversity problems. I have never seen a team of non-managerial people working on a tough ethnic problem fail to produce a response that was both sensitive and effective. The disasters come when managers and officers, or the legal department, get involved and attempt to make decisions that others must carry out. Often the managers seek only to prevent litigation and negative publicity. The non-managerial group seeks solutions that will allow the successful resumption of work in a way that will prevent the problem from repeating, but without a loss of ethnic or cultural identity or respect. Those outcomes are the most basic goals of the empowerment movement.

From Cultural Boundaries to Functional Identities

Psychologically, it is sound to suggest that one result of the traditional corporate rejection of cultural differences is the strengthening of informal, non-corporate cultural identification. Often when a human need (such as cultural affiliation) is denied or ignored within the formal communication system, the need will be met within the informal system. If an effective team member is asked to identify the ethnic identities within their work team, a detailed and accurate response is easily offered. This shift in communication systems from the formal to the informal is a long-accepted, well-documented practice in the majority of U.S. organizations.

Psychologically, it is a short and reasonable jump from informally slotting people into cultural groups to informally putting them in functional groups from which personal identities are assigned. The most obvious result of this segmentation is the traditional boundaries that exist between the technical and nontechnical employees. Virtually everyone in any organization can tell you clearly about the differences between "techies" and "people people." The labels themselves demonstrate the identities.

Once the switch to fully functional, empowered work teams is commenced, those old identities present serious barriers within the team. The most effective leaders of successful transitions see the team as a marriage between technical and nontechnical people and processes. In fact, my experience leads me to believe that the clear technical identities that exist on new teams become gradually less defined as the team members become more comfortable with each other.

New Problem, Old Answer

Not surprisingly, the primary vehicle to support the successful technical/nontechnical marriage is interteam and intrateam communication. There is no other effective way to resolve differences among people than through communication. The old concept of assimilation actually served as a vehicle to avoid communication about differences among people. However, in the transition to a new model that embraces differences and allows the operational-level employees to resolve issues through the evolution of effective teams, the demand for highly skilled leaders and team members who specialize in communications is crucial.

Team-Oriented Responses to Diversity

The most knowledgeable team problem-solving operators will tell you clearly what the primary advantage of diverse workforce is: increased creativity and broader problem-solving perspective. They seek team members who will not look at problems and processes in the same way they've looked at them before. They seek dialogue that explores differences in perceptions. They see those differences as opportunities to find new answers and approaches.

Peter Senge has moved to the forefront of American thought about the nature of the truly effective working organization. His book, *The Fifth Discipline*, fully develops the concept of "the learning organization," which establishes that the only effective organizations are those that can learn fast and put those learnings into action quickly. Senge's lectures rivet audiences with the often paradoxical notion that decision making in many Japanese companies seems to take much longer than it does in U.S. companies, yet the Japanese get more done and constantly improve their processes to achieve this. He resolves this dilemma by demonstrating that the key to decision making in Japanese companies is to bring the decision-making process to the staff levels who are most affected by the problem. Rewards for this kind of decision making are often tied to finding a new way to get a job done rather than for blind adherence to existing practices.

The TQM approach to diversity is captured in seeking highly creative improvements to existing practices. Naive questions are encouraged and answers to naive questions are thought out carefully and completely. A diverse team can accomplish these explorations more completely than a homogeneous cultural or ethnic group.

Diverse groups often seek to find commonalities among themselves. Often these commonalities relate to issues of quality, excellence, dignity, and respect. Agreement about how hard to work, standards of excellence, and groundrules of group interaction, all increase the likelihood of positive performance. Once a diverse group has sought and found its own commonalities, then differences are not only encouraged, they are celebrated. When I was working as manufacturing purchasing agent, the plant manager, a man not especially renowned for interpersonal sensitivity, explained that one of the reasons our plant had very little labor unrest was because each department was clearly aware of its various ethnic identities. He explained that each nationality was acknowledged by each other nationality within each team, and the differences were respected and encouraged. Later, when I was attending graduate school and still working in the plant, I tested his hypothesis through a series of interviews with workers about diversity awareness for a course project. Virtually every man and woman in a workforce of more than one hundred knew the ethnic origin of every other employee. At no time did any employee describe any other group, either racially or ethnically, in disrespectful terms. Often positive work behaviors were seen as related to the values held by national or ethnic groups. The Lithuanian man who worked in the polishing area was credited for having the high standards, bordering on fastidiousness, needed to meet the demanding specifications of his job. Many of the people I spoke to believed those standards were directly related to his Lithuanian culture. Equally clear in many of those interviews was the assertion that this acute cultural awareness and respect was not the result of any formal attempt from the company management to achieve it but rather the outcome of a group of people who had figured out that their work was simply easier without a lot of interpersonal conflict resulting from the differences among them.

The Liabilities of Co-Existence

For those companies who seek to make a successful transition from traditional hierarchic thought and practice to the operational philosophies of team-oriented decision making, the effective response to diversity among the workforce is a delicate and careful one. If current personnel policies are still tied to assimilative concepts, then the idea of encouraging active demonstration of cultural differences will surely violate those policies. From hiring to orientation practices, an often subtle resistance exists that not only squashes celebration of differences, but prevents anything except homogeneity from the start.

Even when workers do have cultural and ethnic differences, how they should behave relative to those differences can present a very confusing set of choices. The idea that an Asian worker, for example, serving on an empowered team is encouraged to talk about, educate others about, and generally celebrate his Asian identity to facilitate a richer approach to problem solving may be safe behavior only when he is working on that team. If he also has non-team duties of a traditional nature, he may find that he must behave far differently in that role. He is presented with a bizarre sort of organizational schizophrenia, which is very demanding in terms of control skills and potentially insulting to him each time his ethnic values must be ignored.

Even more demanding, in terms of remarkable control and social skills, is what is required of his supervisor, who could also end up as his team leader. The highly supportive coaching and coordinating skills that he or she must develop to truly embrace the team leadership role become even more demanding when we add the sensitivity skills needed to encourage diverse identities among team members.

It is a well-documented fact that decision-making transitions take the greatest toll on middle management due jointly to reduced need for the traditional "cop" role and the difficulty of learning a whole new approach to leading others. That difficulty is increased through the expectation that leaders will adequately respond to diversity issues among their teams. It is hard enough for many people to make this change once. When the expectation that this supervisor switch back and forth between the traditional supervisor's roles and these newer leadership roles is added, only a small percentage of management can tolerate such a tug of war. Subsequently, the structures by which those supervisors are evaluated and rewarded usually fall short of the mark to help supervisors develop new approaches. The potential is bleak, but there are ways to make the process workable.

Solutions

First, executives and key leaders must work to eliminate the fear of diversity that grips the majority of the managers in their organizations. Fear of diversity *is not* an automatic result of traditional hierarchic operations. The example of the manufacturing environment as well as the solutions in the foundry mentioned previously indicate that people can and will resolve their own problems arising from differences. The organizations where I have seen diversity awareness encouraged have not had to sponsor detailed programs mandated from the executive levels. They have instead simply sanctioned frank interventions from managers and supervisors who sought to develop a smoothly flowing work process. Potential conflict among people was resolved rather than avoided. Differences were defined in positive terms. Let anyone describe his or her own ethnic, racial, or religious characteristics and they will do so in a positive way. Even when they are self-critical, they will do so humorously and respectfully. So the primary solution to overcoming the fear and resistance to diverse differences within any organization is to let people alone to solve such problems in a way that satisfies their own need for self-respect and dignity. Letting them alone means encouraging them to express their cultural identity without mandated restrictions or punishment.

Second, for the environments where those behaviors have been extinguished by corporate mandates, front-line managers can work as communication liaisons and coaches to allow employees to recapture their own solutions. In addition there are hundreds of programs and specialists who can help increase the level and effectiveness of diversity awareness. Federal grants and other programs from government and civic groups are available to companies who sincerely want to change their corporate response to diversity issues.

The Asset of Diversity 37

This attempt to reduce or eliminate the fear of diversity must be more than programs, however. We have all seen the results of the latest fad initiative around which all senior managers rally with lots of press, arm bands, mandated awareness programs, and other forms of demonstrated "commitment." Most company veterans know how to respond to these flashes of fanatical, intense energy. They simply say and do whatever they need to avoid appearing resistant and then, once the furor dies down, go back to life as they knew it previously. The primary step in the process to remove the fear of diversity is through example. When the executive council of any large corporation announces its next big initiative to remedy the gender imbalance, for example, and that council is exclusively male, the real message will not be lost to the employees, especially the women. The countless examples within the federal government over the years of highly visible, highly funded programs to ensure diversity hiring, while whole agencies such as the FBI or IRS often ignored them in their own practices is an easy demonstration that modeling provides the true test of sincerity. For many companies that have yet to deal adequately with gender imbalance, or racial imbalance, the idea of insisting that executives model behaviors embracing culturally different ideas and people seems far in the future. Yet among those few organizations that have had a relatively successful record in this arena, the one consistent behavior seems to be modeling at the top.

The concept of modeling also encompasses the appointment of representatives of new groups in the workforce within the executive ranks, senior teams with the authority to create and implement policy and *then* sponsorship of organization-wide initiatives to raise awareness and respect of differences among people. Once the CEO at the foundry mentioned previously added both Indian and Portuguese people, male and female, to the ranks of senior executives and then formed a team of those executives to improve diversity awareness. The end result was far more realistic and applicable to the work lives of the front-line workers. Executive management of a broad-based approach to diversity requires truly visionary leadership skills. This carefully planned process is easily joined and blended with the detailed communication plan. This plan should be at the forefront of every transition initiative.

A second solution to issues of diversity awareness is to rely on the built-in philosophy of acceptance, which is often already established and functional among the hourly workforce in most companies. Perhaps the most powerful results I have seen in my consulting work among companies that have tried to move to a new plateau of acceptance and encouragement of diverse groups has come from those that have created teams assigned to create a path to that plateau. A cross-departmental, multi-level team of people dedicated to involving the entire workforce in the potential celebration of human differences is an effective demonstration of recursiveness at its best.

Several sub-issues can be spawned from such a diversity approach. A group charged with creation of new policies to respond to cultural and ethnic diversity, if properly led, can produce remarkably clear results. As diversity issues become more accepted and supported throughout the total organization, the disparity between what is tolerated inside and outside an empowered team is reduced. What remains as necessary differences are easily managed by a group whose job it is to identify the differences and establish behavioral guidelines for each role.

Ultimately, all successful approaches to utilizing the potential advantages of an ethnically and culturally diverse workforce while minimizing the disadvantages requires proactive leadership. The traditional models of reactionary response which have been our primary models simply will not work within a true TQM, reengineering, or change philosophy. When organizational leaders are willing to explore new approaches based on involving all groups in the exploration, the potential to create highly effective solutions is assured.

THREE

People Are the Cause, Tools, and Effect

The procedural, mechanical side of TQM was designed by technical experts. Perhaps the power of the system is that it closely parallels many previous structural approaches to problem solving. Yet, whenever a TQM or reengineering effort fails or gets bogged down and loses steam, the explanation seldom includes a lack of adequate technical knowledge needed to make the change effective. The practices that demonstrate the philosophies are not hard to follow or to learn. More often the reasons for ineffective transition initiatives relate to the human side of the process.

Managers or sponsors often do not realize the difficulties involved in teaching their employees a whole new way to think about work. They fail to see that the real secret to survival is in the degree to which leaders can demonstrate the demanding and flexible interpersonal skills needed for a successful transition. That, coupled with an acute sense of the differences between the status quo of hierarchial management and the often untamed wilderness of the new philosophy is crucial. Too often transition leaders stress the technical knowledge as the real message when in fact the technical aspect is a way to think about getting work done.

The understanding transition initiators who have not truly grasped the essence of the empowerment factor within the new philosophy comes when they finally realize that this movement is about people, not programs, technology, or tools. Not until senior level managers and executives have accepted that the very nature of the work their organization does is up for grabs, with new, highly effective ways to operate as the payoff, can the training programs, technology, and tools be used effectively. Sometimes the outcomes of empowerment, especially at the beginning of the transition, can be surprising. One of the first requests of the newly formed quality teams at Taylor and Fenn, the foundry with whom I have worked for many years, was to eliminate the reserved parking places for managers and arrange parking on a first-come, first-served basis. Because many of the foundry's hourly force started work very early, this arrangement provided them with a clear advantage over managers for parking closest to the building. The management team felt that this request was a test of their commitment. No one pretended that the request was closely related to the quality requirements that teams were supposed to be addressing, yet management felt that refusing the request would set a bad precedent. So they agreed to the request with a few minor revisions (like assurance that visitors would be accommodated), and all but one senior manager gave up the reserved parking place.

At the same time, the quality teams began to focus on important issues like reducing scrap rates and increasing casting process turnaround times with remarkable and permanent results. Once the rank and file began to see clear demonstrations of commitment to the shift in power and decision making, they began to look seriously at the current processes and naturally knew where and how to improve.

The real secret to transitioning to an empowered, self-directed work force lies in a rare marriage of skills within the leadership of the change. In addition to a fully operational understanding of the discipline of the TQM technology and structures, leaders must also possess an equally operational set of interpersonal, organizational, and team-oriented skills to help participants bridge the gap between the incompatible philosophies of traditional hierarchy and team-oriented decision making. To suggest that such a marriage of skills is very rare in organizations today is a gross understatement. But for those companies that have capable leaders or are interested in developing them, the payoffs include state of the art practices and innovations which may spell stability and enhanced competitiveness in the years ahead.

The following is a chart of the two different sets of knowledge and skills employed in the TQM/reengineering transition process. The intent in the use of these basic steps to transition is to illustrate the flow of logic inherent in the process. The corresponding human-interaction skills associated with each of the structural steps represents my experience studying and observing transition initiatives in several different organizations and industries.

KEY INITIATIVE OWNERSHIP	STRUCTURAL/ TECHNICAL STEPS (TOOLS)	INTERACTIVE SKILLS AND TECHNIQUES
	1. Delineate broad initiative to Team Leader, presented in terms of desirable out-comes related to clear business goals. (Leadership Development)	Clear conceptualizing and communication skills. Ability to select and recruit the right leadership. Ability to describe goal in outcome format without implicit or explicit solutions.

KEY INITIATIVE OWNERSHIP	STRUCTURAL/ TECHNICAL STEPS (TOOLS)	INTERACTIVE SKILLS AND TECHNIQUES
Sponsor's Roles and Responsibilities.	2. Work with Team Leader to identify core team members.	Motivational skills. Political skills for successful recruitment. Clear conceptual communication skills.
	3. Meet with team to give broad charge and discuss behavioral parameters (Establishing A Clear Vision).	Establishment of autonomous identity of team. Clear shift in authority to team leader and team members. Specialized communication skills — general, conceptual yet clear.
	4. Team meets to pick focused issue and set operational ground rules.	Team building skills. Initial firm control without autocracy. Encouragement toward autonomy and personal creativity.
Team Leader's Roles and Responsibilities.	5. Team gathers facts and data about current problem situation. (Data Gathering and Display Methods)	Dealing with opinions and desire for quick fix. Patience and persistence. Ability to think and project ahead of the group.
	6. Team uses researched data to assess and evaluate current problem and creates focused problem statement. (Process Flow Charts and Process Mapping)	Team conflict management skills. Interpersonal problem solving skills. Group facilitation skills without imposing leader's outcomes or solutions.
	7. Team uses facts and data to determine primary causes of current problem. (Ishakawa Diagrams)	Brainstorming skills. Challenging assumptions.

KEY INITIA-TIVE OWN-ERSHIP	STRUCTURAL/ TECHNICAL STEPS (TOOLS)	INTERACTIVE SKILLS AND TECHNIQUES
	8. Team brainstorms possible improvements for each primary cause. (Force Field Analysis)	Stimulating creativity skills. Pushing team beyond initial solution. Supporting team members whose original ideas are no longer viable. Communication to target areas affected by the new process.
	9. Team designs and implements a pilot improvement test.	Sales skills with management of pilot area. Transition skills to take team from owners of process to objective observers and evaluators.
Transfer of Responsibility From Team To Line Management.	10. Team assesses test results against original objectives and customer demands	Objectivity modeling. Disciplined adherence to objectives. Amplifying the voice of the customer. Expanded communication to entire organization.
	11. Improvement plan is revised and may be retested.	Patience modeling.
	12. Improvement is rolled out to entire organization.	Expanding line management buy-in and commitment. Team transition skills to relinquish ownership of solutions.
	13. Team serves as consultants and experts.	Collaborative consulting-skill building for team members.
	14. Team returns next improvement, accepts new assignment, or disbands.	Refocusing team. Evaluating team process and individuals. Identifying new leaders or designing leadership-development plans for promising candidates. Potentially ending team and transitioning back to original assignments and structures.

Group Interaction Requirements

Initial Phase

When presented with the need during the transition for clear communication skills, leaders often view those skills as purely personal behaviors used to make others understand or to understand others. Although those communication skills are paramount for leaders, what is often missing in the definition of communication skills is a broader picture. Communication skills for transition leaders include answering questions, such as,: What exactly should we tell the people in various departments who will be affected by the transition? What will we tell the people who will not be affected, at least initially, by the transition? Who should tell them? When should they be told? How much do they need to know? What is the most effective method to ensure they get the message? How will we gather feedback about the impact of our plan on their production? Do we tell people outside the team about the wonderful cohesiveness of our team or only about the results that will impact their lives?

Unfortunately, many ideas of traditional hierarchy include communication "rules" that are extremely destructive to the values of empowerment. There are still leaders in America who believe that workers should be given only enough information to follow directions correctly. Because independent decision making was never the responsibility of the general worker, the information flow needed to support such decision making was never a part of the communication pipeline.

In the transition process, information of the broadest nature must be disseminated to the very base of the organization if intelligent decisions are to follow. It is usually a short time before the word "communication" is replaced with the word "trust."

Are the leaders of the transition ready to trust their own workforce with the full long-range plan for the organization? Are they ready to say that the five-year plan shows a company with a workforce reduced by 40%? The most fundamental beliefs about the capability of the workforce to deal with full information are brought kicking and screaming into the light of day, and they must be resolved at the very top before an effective communication plan can be designed and implemented.

My experience with companies planning a transition is that the leadership seldom addresses the fundamental beliefs around full communication. This style of communication is so far from traditional beliefs and behaviors about the dissemination of information that its importance is often overlooked by the sponsor. It is often left to the transition leader to encourage the sponsor to devise a communication plan prior to setting the transition in motion.

Highly functional individual communication skills are essential throughout the entire initiative, regardless of phase or ownership. At the first stages of a TQM/reengineering assignment, those communication skills require highly specialized listening techniques. As the intended team leader enters into a series of direction and clarity meetings with the program sponsor, the leader must work like a consultant or counselor would to clarify the messages of the sponsor. Often the sponsor views the change initiative as a solution to an existing problem or as insurance against an impending problem. The leader's job is to try not to jump to a solution, but rather try to fully understand the problem.

At the earliest stages of the process, it is not uncommon for the leader to meet with senior executives whose various functions are impacted by the problem and the potential solutions. Where such a group is part of the direction planning, the group interaction skills are vital and often most lacking. Issues of territory protection, assessing blame, and potential control of the initiative often impede effective communication and make the message to the team leader confused and unclear.

Recently, I was invited to facilitate a meeting of senior executives whose collective job it was to assign the task of a cross-functional team representing each of their functions to solve a longstanding divisional problem. The group had met twice before with the team leader, who had asked that I facilitate the third meeting because the first two were so unclear and frustrating. When the group gathered, the feeling of conflict and tension among most of them was evident. There was no opening small talk, people chose their respective seats carefully, no one welcomed or introduced me, or offered any background information.

I began by asking each person to introduce themself and within that introduction to state how the problem impacted their function and to share their perception of the problem. After the first three (of eight) participants spoke, it was clear that no one accepted any responsibility for the problem and that no one in the room was listening to anyone else's explanations. After listening to each participant explain away their potential involvement with the causes of the problem and hearing each person's frustration with their own failed attempts to get others to own the problem, I decided to try to alter the communication system among this group. I asked the group if they felt they had adequately understood each other's perception of the problem. They nodded their affirmation. I then asked each person to mentally change seats with the person to their right and to restate the problem from that person's point of view to the satisfaction of that person. The results served two important purposes. First, it made the group laugh to hear how feebly they were able to state each other's opinions, and, second, it forced them to listen.

Next, I asked each person to write down as many ways as they could think of that their department contributed to the problem within the last six months. At first, nobody was writing. Then the senior executive of the group began to write, and soon everybody was hard at work listing their behaviors contributing to the problem. The intended outcome of this meeting was to provide the TQM leader with a clear understanding of the need for the initiative. Now, perhaps for the first time, the executive leaders were accepting responsibility jointly for the current situation. The fundamental skills of clear message sending and active, nonjudgmental listening play a key role for groups in any stage of the transition process.

Nearly any well-planned communication skills class will cover the fundamentals of listening, message clarity, questioning or probing, and giving and receiving feedback. The need for these skills in transition leaders and sponsors isn't merely a nice idea. It is an essential requirement. Solid communication skills will compensate for other weaknesses because they can serve as the means to access the skills of others.

There is also a demanding series of group interactions among the members of the newly forming TQM team. This group is usually formed around a core of people who are intimately involved in the current situation. Although the team leader is responsible for clearly delivering the charge to this core group, the group members, many of whom already work together, must agree to start this process fresh. This includes the establishment of ground rules that may conflict with previous ways of working together. Each team member needs to feel secure that their skills and knowledge will still serve them adequately in the new group environment. A rather stormy formation period also may occur, which requires a healthy dose of faith to navigate effectively. Known as the storming phase, savvy leaders recognize that this is a necessary requirement to establish real trust among team members. The leader serves a vital role to help the group work through their differences rather than avoid or ignore them.

Establishing a Complete Focused Team

There continues to be a great deal of research about the development phase of the TQM or reengineering team. What teams needed to do in the past to become effective still proves true in this phase, and the power of the team, when properly facilitated, is the very nucleus of the change philosophy. In addition to established team-building fundamentals, there are also several factors about team problem solving which require special skills and techniques to prevent the deterioration of interaction within the team.

Recently an associate and I jointly delivered a series of sessions collectively called PROGRESS, a program we purchased from the Forum Corporation that offered a TQM methodology and discipline. The clients were a group of young people who worked in the mail service process at a financial services company. As we started working they were neither motivated nor excited to learn about a new way to work together. As we led them through the steps of the PROGRESS program, they began to realize that they would be expected to solve a process problem on their own, without traditional management directives. Once they felt safe that they were not being set up to fail they swung full circle and became extremely excited about their own potential to think and work independently.

Their excitement began to wane, however, when they found themselves embroiled in a five-way argument about the cause of the problem was and what they should do about it. Because they worked together every day anyway, their patterns of communication, their knowledge of each others' capabilities, and their individual idiosyncracies were well established. They were uninterested in working differently even though they complained about their interactive work process. It took three long slow meetings for this team to work into a new way to function, in addition to professional outside facilitation. But the payoff surprised everyone, especially their managers. Once they began to search for facts about the problem, rather than rely on individual opinions about the problem and solutions, they uncovered several other weak processes related to their own work and began to generate exciting, realistic, and creative approaches to improving the entire mail services process. More important, they each developed a whole new attitude about work, which others might have thought impossible given their experience and education.

The key to unlocking the potential of any established group is to recognize that the existing patterns of interaction must be identified and changed if they present obstacles to the team's ability to discover new behaviors and ways to interact.

Those new behaviors include supporting the ideas and opinions of various team members, especially when those ideas represent a break from traditional logic or operations. It is likely, especially at the start of a TQM initiative, that individuals will state forceful opinions about the problem or demand that their solutions be implemented before any real data has been gathered in support. Team leadership must encourage and insist that every member of the team be accepting of other team members. Often these tolerance behaviors are difficult for some team members to summon. Unless the team developed support behaviors prior to the team assignment, special attention needs to be paid to the development of new support behaviors.

Team leaders are often strongly results-focused at the beginning of a transition, and the need to go a bit slower is difficult for them to meet. When team leaders have been adequately trained, or own the natural skills to do so, an important step is added which focuses exclusively on the interpersonal communication process within the team. To step away from the results focus and use new problem-solving skills to solve interpersonal conflict will pay off later when real differences of opinion will become valuable assets to the team in the creation of new ideas and improvements.

Transfer of Initiative to Line Management

Perhaps the most demanding group interaction skill is found in the team's need to shift ownership of the potential improvement to the line operators, with whom it will live permanently. Virtually all of the team's effort thus far has been toward gradually increasing ownership and autonomy regarding the problem and their solutions to improve the process. Team members often feel a strong sense of expertise on the process they've studied and are reluctant to allow outsiders into key roles to make the improvement operational.

For TQM teams who have finally reached the point of conducting a pilot test of their improved process, it is imperative to develop the discipline to leave the pilot test behaviors alone during the test. The team knows exactly what the new behaviors are supposed to accomplish and, as they watch others demonstrate those new behaviors, they are likely to interfere and correct the pilot group's performance if the results are not where the team members think they should be. Naturally this interference causes the results of the pilot to be suspect.

We have had strong success with a classroom exercise for process improvement teams that demonstrates the value and frustration of letting operators alone run the pilot. We divide the group into two teams, one planners and the other operators. The operators are moved to a separate room while the planners are given a complex puzzle. The planners' task is to design the instructions for the operators to assemble the puzzle. The planners have a blueprint for the desired outcome but may not share it with the operators, relying purely on their ability to create clear instructions for the operators. When their planning time is up, operators return to the room and planners have five minutes to explain the instructions. The operators may not touch the puzzle pieces until the instructions are given. Once the operators touch the pieces the planners may not add any additional instructions, guidance, or coaching. After the intense and often frenzied time the planners have spent to design the perfect instructions, it is difficult for them to remain calm during the construction of the puzzle by the operators. It is not uncommon that members of both groups are moved to tears by the frustration of incomplete instructions or simply incorrect behavior. Both groups take the success or failure of the endeavor very seriously, and the debrief after the exercise is extremely valuable as a way to understand a useful pilot. Ultimately, the team will learn from the mistakes of the pilot and will improve their product accordingly.

The group interaction skills to restrain the desire to fix the pilot in-process can be very demanding. It is sometimes after-the-fact that the group realizes they contaminated the pilot results and need to rerun it. They often need to agree on exact parameters of pilot behavior that allow necessary interference, usually related to the safety of the pilot operators.

The ability to leave the pilot operators' behavior alone can be elusive for some teams.

In addition to the ownership issues of this final phase, the natural desire to be finished with the project sometimes makes it hard for the team to get motivated to start the process over and repeat it with the next improvement. The issues of "cleansing" old habits and assumptions before the group begins again becomes more difficult when the previous behaviors were largely successful and empowering to group members. The feeling among the team that they "know how to do this now" can often be as much of a liability as an asset when it prevents the team from improving their working systems and groundrules.

Evaluating the Initiative

My experience working with new transition teams has enabled me to find a common weakness when the team is too focused on the problem and its potential solutions. Teams that stress the bottom line exclusively often have no adequate measures to evaluate their own process once the project is over. Too often the evaluation is an analysis to determine whether the problem has gone away. Team members have not gathered data along the way to learn whether their problem-solving process was efficient, their schedule was optimum, or the customer is satisfied with the process to achieve the improved behavior.

I once worked with a product design team whose job was to create products for field employees to use in assessing the safety needs of their customers. As the safety engineers in the field would respond to the demands and challenges of their customers, they would look back to their home office for new products and procedures that would assist them.

I was amazed to see the detail with which this team, comprised primarily of design engineers would go to in their efforts to respond to field requests. They not only designed exceptionally well-made products, they also supported those products with volumes of background data and instructions. It was not uncommon for the team to send cases of paperwork to the field for engineers to refer to as they applied the new products. Over the years, the evaluation of this team was determined largely by whether the new products and support information got out to the field in a reasonable amount of time. Not much evaluation was done to learn if the field engineers actually used the products or support information. Given the chance to talk to a few field engineers, I found that while they had great respect and admiration for the product design team's ability and thoroughness, they seldom used the new products and almost never used the support materials. This was because the material simply was not offered to them in a format that made sense. These people were constantly on the go, and working out of their cars or from hotel rooms. In other words, the system to evaluate whether the team was meeting its objectives was not user oriented but product oriented. Once we began to help the team concentrate more on its customers, the field engineers, the entire process by which the team set their objectives changed. They also were able to evaluate the entire team process from both a product and a process point of view.

The primary responsibility for an effective evaluative plan belongs to the team leader. The data needed to evaluate the entire team experience must be determined before the project begins, and it must be communicated to the team throughout the process. The team itself also owns an interactive responsibility to maintain the discipline to constantly evaluate and measure every aspect of the improvement process. The process improvement system that the new decision-making approach defines thus must be recursive within the actual improvement process.

Fuel for the Engines of Change

Perhaps the largest, most inclusive determinant of failed transitions can be generalized into the topic of inadequate communications. The requirements for clear copious communication to facilitate a gradual or even an abrupt change in decision making cannot be overestimated.

In the Introduction, concept of effective transition communication is divided into two requirements of transition leaders. These are intra-team communication and team-nonteam communication. In order to minimize the resistance, which is a natural reaction to change, a detailed plan for communication is required.

At the top of the transition leadership team, a stringent requirement exists to decide who should know what about the intended outcomes of the transition, when they should know it, and what communication vehicles should be utilized to convey the message. Once the initial transition process has begun, each team must include in its structure the requirement of communication, both from a content and a process viewpoint.

Closely aligned with the organizational requirement is a need for clarity about desired outcomes and schedules. It has a profoundly different impact on workers to be told that the company is undertaking a huge, elaborate initiative to reduce the new product design turnaround time than to tell them that, by January 15th, we will have completed a process of improvement which will result in a new, abbreviated product turnaround time. Over the course of my years as an organizational consultant, I have seen what workers can accomplish once they know exactly what the desired outcome is and once they believe it is in their own best interests to pursue it.

I once sat in on a plant manager's talk with a group of senior machinists to get their buy-in to a demanding production schedule to build the largest, most complex machine in the company's product line. Especially significant in this presentation was the unique situation that when they finished this machine the plant would close forever, and they would all become unemployed. The plant manager was clear and his message had a certain simplicity which was very effective. He explained that if they did not reach the deadline to deliver the machine on time, they would be in default of their contract and the company would not be able to invoice the customer. Without that last invoice, the company would be unable to pay the severance agreements each employee was entitled to under the terms of their contract. While the union could probably sue for the severance, the resolution of the suit would be some distance in the future. It seemed to the plant manager that the machinists would need their severance immediately after the plant closed in order to have time to find new jobs. Once the machinists were convinced that this was a financial reality and not an idle threat, they went to work and made the deadline with two days to spare.

Nothing is more frustrating to a hard working employee than to have his or her work discounted or devalued by a constantly changing set of expectations and goals. People can deal with all sorts of rapid process changes without a great deal of travail but only when the overall goals and expectations remain relatively constant.

FOUR

Leading the Discipline of Transition

In Chapter Three, the exploration of the interactive requirements for transition team were explored as they correspond with the standard steps of a typical problem-solving initiative. It is difficult to separate the requirements of the team from the requirements of the team leader because the team developmental concept is so dynamic, causing synergistic results that can be credited to both the group and the leader, but to neither separately. Yet, if we can isolate the demands placed on the team leader in terms of knowledge of the sequential, technical steps of the process and the complex requirements of team building and communication, it is possible to capture the vital role of an effective transition leader.

This Chapter will utilize the same model as Chapter Three—the sequence of typical steps of the human interactive requirements, specifically from the view of the leader. The result is the creation of a leadership profile that is intensely demanding. The "new leadership" identity that corresponds with the development of effective transition practices is an elusive one.

In 1987, Tom Peters set out to create a new training video that would showcase truly effective leaders who have moved their organizations into an atmosphere of empowerment and continuous improvement. What he found were leaders who had a remarkable combination of hard-nosed business skills coupled with a nearly intuitive sense for how people really want to work. The video, *The Leadership Alliance*, didn't show solo stars but people whose faith in teamwork and in people is truly inspirational.

We know that new leaders have emerged and are continuing to emerge. The development of such leaders is a highly eclectic process. Some, like Ralph Stayer at Johnsonville Foods, used a highly intuitive, almost metaphysical path while others, like Vaughn Beals at Harley Davidson, simply evolved to the role by having exhausted the alternatives. In every case, regardless of the manner in which the end was achieved, the one commonality appears to be a desire to work effectively with groups of people and then allow those people to control their own work processes. The knowledge, techniques, and skills required to make it all happen are available for us to study and even practice. But the real challenge for leaders is to find a unique blend of those elements which will fit within the already existing cultures of their hierarchical organizations.

Thinking the Philosophy

The philosophy behind the quality/reengineering movement is much more than a series of steps to follow to solve problems. Companies that have tried to adopt these practices without a full understanding of the basic values and beliefs that are embodied within the practices have sooner or later failed, often with devastating effects on resources and people.

As covered previously, trying to move a large financial services corporation to team decision-making practices without a clear understanding of the drastic shift in philosophy and values was a costly and frustrating mistake. The culture of the financial services industry was (and is) not based on the values inherent in the empowerment philosophy. That is not to say that such a shift is impossible. It means instead that the values and basic tenets must be in place if the movement is to stay focused on performance and success.

Fueling the Communication Pipeline

If we combine the two large requirements of full philosophical understanding at the top and a fully effective communication effort used to lead the changes, we can eliminate the serious mistake that some organizations make as they try to slide carefully into empowered, operational mind-sets. Too often they begin the process in an experimental mode and say so through the communication system. Such an attempt is dangerous unless the communication system is planned very carefully. The obvious danger is that the experimental message can easily be perceived as lack of full management commitment and understanding.

The process of communication, especially at the beginning of a transition effort, is more important than the effort itself. What information people have to work with is important, but seldom do organizations realize that how they get it is often more powerful than the information itself. Within the adult education and training business, the concept of recursiveness is a vital part of any effective change strategy. Recursiveness is defined as the ability to have the process of learning actually demonstrate the content of the learning. For example, it is much more likely to produce effective results for a class on team-building to be set up in small team clusters and activities than it is to handle the content in standard lecture format with the audience seated in rows.

Nowhere is the idea of recursiveness more important than in the communication process organizations use to lead a team-centered transition. The concept of using teams to accomplish nearly all work should result in communicated messages about transitions coming from teams and presented jointly as the result of team efforts. Once executives and senior managers begin to realize the power of the communication process, as opposed to its content, they are more likely to share their strategy as the product of an executive-team effort. The communication process can then begin with a recursive model of the actual content the executive team wishes to communicate.

A continuation of this concept can consist of initial messages from the top, focused more on outcomes and less on process, while announcing the creation of key teams assigned to plan a process to get the transition into operation. People need to have input into changes that affect their jobs if they are to develop commitment to new behaviors. The new process is based on that input requirement, and smart transition leaders realize that the system and process of early communication can actually demonstrate the outcomes they seek. In some smaller companies or divisions, the transition process begins with each department selecting a person to represent the group on a team charged to plan an effective communication process for the new initiative. While this communication planning team may only exist for a short time early on, the modeling it represents has value far behind its lifespan.

Fundamental Values and Basic Beliefs

Much has been written about the primary values of the team-centered, decision-making approach. Here is a short summary of some of those beliefs that relate most closely to the interactive requirements for TQM team leaders.

Effective TQM leaders believe that:

- People at every level of the workforce can and will embrace clear business objectives designed to ensure the success of the organization, and that they can make sound business decisions consistent with those objectives.

- Most decisions do not need to be made by the leader if the workers are aware of what is important, and that those important things relate to their own security and survival needs, as well as the organization's.

- Given adequate trust among members, teams can make sound decisions related to the most difficult problems, including decisions about the workforce size, skill requirements, compensation, and security.

- Accountability for proper decision making can rest completely with a well-informed, properly developed team and need not be held exclusively by the leaders.

When viewed by many current executives and managers of large U.S. corporations, these beliefs are considered radical. Yet those same people can cite examples in other organizations where those values work, such as churches, community groups, and sports teams. They simply don't see them as viable for profit-oriented workplaces. Frequently they are being proven wrong.

Balancing the Technical with the Human

The most demanding requirements for leaders in a philosophy transition do not fall exclusively into one category of technical or human interaction, but are found in the combination of both. Perhaps the rarity of leaders who possess the full array of skills to achieve longlasting success in this transitional mode comes from the profound differences between the technical and the human interaction.

Recently, while conducting a new problem-solving awareness session with a group of design engineers in the field of manufacturing safety, one of the participants announced that he was pleased at last, we had a way to improve performance without having "to worry about all that touchy-feely crap." He was thrilled that the system I had just shown him was technically sound and well thought out, and his analytical mind knew it would work. Unfortunately, he offered his revelation before I had completed the session. Naturally, I had saved the hardest piece for last. When he learned that effective team building was the true key to success, he was disgusted and very resistant. No explanation of the need for human interactive involvement would satisfy him. If we needed to worry about how people felt and interacted to get the job done, he was convinced that the plan would fail. Sadly, if he was leading such a plan it would fail, and he would never see why.

The other side of the coin is equally problematic. We have seen team leaders chosen for their people skills who lack the necessary knowledge and discipline to carry out the detailed approach, which is required for teams to solve problems on their own.

Leading the Discipline of Transition

Perhaps the time within the problem solving process that requires the most leadership discipline comes when a team has selected an improvement process and are pilot testing the new behaviors. We have seen leaders who so want the pilot to be successful and validate the hard work of the team, that the leader allows or even encourages team members to enter the pilot test and alter the plan in mid-test, thereby contaminating the pilot test data and causing confusion about which behaviors to save for the full improvement roll-out.

Clearly, a balance is needed. The following is a chart derived from the chart in Chapter Three that demonstrates the parallel skill set that effective transition leaders must possess if they are to be successful:

TECHNICAL SKILLS	HUMAN INTERACTION SKILLS
1. Developing clear understanding of the assignment from sponsor.	Developing trust with sponsor. Probing and researching without causing defensiveness.
2. Selecting and developing a team with sponsor assistance and support. Assessing technical requirements to meet apparent project outcomes.	Selecting and recruiting members on the basis of team and social skills. Modeling those skills to potential team members.
3. Focusing new team on the problem to improve without suggesting solutions. Descriptions of needed outcomes.	Developing a functional team quickly and effectively. Leading team to establish groundrules and accept responsibility for interpersonal behavior among team members.
4. Insistence that the team research the problem situation thoroughly before jumping to solutions. Insistence on facts and data to support research.	Allowing the group to express opinions about the problem without judgement. Keeping the team motivated while they gather data about the situation. Encouraging the team to learn new tools.

TECHNICAL SKILLS

HUMAN INTERACTION SKILLS

5. On the basis of research, leader helps team focus on detailed, highly specific issue to improve. Rigorous analysis needed to validate choice.

   Continual challenge to team to improve internal team process. Highly likely that group conflict will require strong facilitation skills to prevent deterioration of positive team identity.

6. Specialized problem analysis skills to lead team through cause and effect diagrams, brainstorming techniques, creativity skills. Continual insistence on researched facts and data to validate all group conclusions.

   As team resolves conflicts and learns about members assets and liabilities, leader assesses capabilities and, when appropriate, gradually begins shift to autonomous control and direction.

7. Team isolates primary causes of the problem and begins to brainstorm ways to reduce each cause. Leader uses specialized skills in problem solving.

   While continuing to challenge team to resolve interpersonal differences, leader also continues to encourage independent decision-making. Keeps team focused on original goals and intended outcomes.

8. Leader helps team choose most likely improvement for pilot test. Leader begins working outside team with pilot area management to assure cooperation.

   Team now works primarily without leadership. Leader becomes team advocate to ensure transition to pilot management without loss of team control on new behavior. Highly specialized coordination skills to bridge between energized team members and potentially resistant line management, whose behavior must change.

9. Pilot test is ready to be run. Leader must model exceptional empirical skills to let pilot run without team interference. Leader must help group resist the desire to force correct results from pilot.

   New roles for team members as process experts and consultants to line pilot-test performers. Requires leader to coach team to begin to let go of the operation of the project. Continual leadership of team evaluative process and developmental coaching to team members for next possible projects.

Leading the Discipline of Transition

TECHNICAL SKILLS	HUMAN INTERACTION SKILLS
10. Pilot data must be evaluated objectively. Leader reapplies skills and tools from earlier steps to display and analyze pilot data. Leader helps team decide next steps—retest, scrap pilot data, prepare full new-behavior roll-out. Rigorous discipline to adhere to original goals and customer demands.	Leader relies on team trust to evaluate pilot data objectively. Constant reminders to adhere to original goals, team groundrules and evaluations. Also continues to prepare team to let go of the control of the project. Possibility that team may have to start over on technical process if pilot fails. Specialized skills to maintain team motivation.
11. Leader works with team and line management to prepare full functional roll-out. Leader must have detailed clarity of original goals and intent to allow translation to real-world application of solution, without loss of essence of original goal.	Continuation of separation of team from project. Leader also begins to dismantle team and coach members to move forward individually. Often works as advocate for specific team members for new projects, more responsibility and potential leadership assignments.
12. Team and leader sign-off project to line management. Team members may serve as ongoing experts to line personnel. Team is dismantled.	Team discontinues work. Leader must effectively close the project and allow members to move on to new projects, or back to previous assignments. Leader may serve as transitional contact to start new team for next assignment and have the flexibility to begin leadership cycle over again.

A review of any leader functioning effectively in the new environment from both the technical discipline and human interactive requirements results in a description of very few people. In addition, current developmental programs available in most universities, training systems, and large human-resource training departments are not yet geared to help individuals develop the skills and insights needed to lead in most of the companies currently in transition. In fact, many large corporations, subjected to downsizing and fiscal belt tightening, are either eliminating their training budgets or drastically reducing the offerings available to managers. Commonly, when management training curricula are reduced, what remains are programs which teach autocratic control and discipline. The prevailing logic seems to be that trusting employees to make sound decisions through involvement in the entire decision-making process is a luxury that can be afforded only when profits are high. However, I believe that the evidence to the contrary strongly opposes such a view point.

Consider the amazing turnaround of Harley-Davidson, the last large U.S. maker of motorcycles. Through the 70s, HD went through a devastating downturn in sales, largely as a result of the gradual deterioration of the quality of their products. By 1977 it was common for Harley-Davidson to ship to dealers, along with the new motorcycles, a piece of monogrammed cardboard to go under the bike on the showroom floor because the manufacturer knew the new bike leaked oil right from the factory. It was decided that it was cheaper to monogram the cardboard and ship it than it was to find and fix the manufacturing process that resulted in the oil leak. By the time Harley-Davidson went to the U.S. government for protection against their creditors (thanks to the precedent established by Chrysler), senior management knew that they would need drastic measures to save the company. As in the case of many of the most dramatic revivals, Harley-Davidson changed to employee involvement and self-managed teams simply because they had tried everything else. They had already tried management by objective, invested millions in elaborate efficiency processes without employee input, and tried all the latest managerial fads. Each quick-fix idea had taken its toll on available resources and not produced adequate results. The one element that HD's senior management had overlooked was the attitude of their workers. A common identity among Harley-Davidson's labor force is that they are all bikers. The parking lot is often more than half filled with motorcycles every day. Once management asked its employees to correct the problems with quality, to find cost effective ways to improve productivity, and to raise the entire bar of performance in the plant, the results were astounding. They began to make immediate huge changes in the quality of the product because the workers knew what quality should look and feel like. Once those same workers were involved in the fiscal planning for their respective areas, they also knew that cost savings had a direct bearing on their own job security. Once the changes to self-management began to really take hold, a new surprising source of cost-cutting became evident. In a few months they reduced their middle management numbers by more than half. There simply was no longer a need for a corps of supervisor-cops whose job was to demand compliance. The results for Harley-Davidson are now a matter of record. They asked to be released from their federal protection a year early, are highly respected in their industry for quality, and are in the forefront in innovation and customer response.

All of this relates to leadership in some relatively radical ways. Traditionally, the idea of letting the labor force make it's own decisions has been associated with soft management, but the stories of effective transition companies is anything but soft. Effective leadership will result in workers who can and will make timely, difficult decisions with surprising precision, once the information which drives those decisions is fairly and honestly placed before them. When people know that every expense impacts their own security or reward directly, they have little regard for performers who do not meet requirements. They will review virtually every practice to ensure its effectiveness and often will tend to over-cut expenses, not undercut.

The role of the leader is to balance the hard data measurement while maintaining a sense of teamwork and trust. It is not surprising that so many transitions fail when we consider the scarcity of such leaders.

As an illustration of the ability of empowered work teams to make tough business decisions, consider the example of Johnsonville Foods. Teams made a decision early on to eliminate all standard pay increases based on seniority or longevity. They decided that increases in pay should be the result of increased skills and contribution to the team's objectives, and that control of those pay increases should belong exclusively to the team.

While tomes have been written about the discipline and technical knowledge that an effective leader must possess to lead a successful transition initiative, aside from casual references to team-building and communication, little has been written about the potentially overwhelming list of people skills needed to lead a team through the interactive maze of such a transition. The previous chart above details some of those skills, and even that attempt falls far short. It is safe to say that most successful transitions will experience a relatively predictable path in terms of problem solving. A view of those same successes will show, however, that the human transition process is not anywhere near as predictable. Not only must a leader possess an impressive array of communication and team-building skills, but the leader must be able to apply them intuitively, tuned to the immediate, changeable, often volatile needs of the team. In addition, the needs for leadership outside the team to ensure successful transfer of the team's work to the host environment, requires a similarly intuitive approach.

In Chapter Five we will focus exclusively on the coordination, political, and cross-over skills that effective transition leadership must possess. These skills are necessary to bridge the contrary worlds of team-centered, operator decision making and hierarchic management.

FIVE

Bridging Two Worlds

While there are hundreds of books and articles on how to operate a TQM organization, or how to conduct a continuous improvement or reengineering process, the much more demanding topic of how to lead a transition, effectively bridging two incompatible philosophies, is largely untouched. The demands for leaders who can function simultaneously in both worlds, while preparing the parent organization to make a permanent shift to new practices, are nearly impossible to meet unless the differences between the two philosophies are understood by the leaders at the top.

Leading such an initiative is often a highly intuitive process. It requires a total knowledge of the intricacies of traditional management systems, coupled with a working knowledge of technical problem-solving and decision-making practices, and the ability to see the impact of one upon the other before the impact occurs. The ability to complete this rabbit-in-the-hat kind of magic requires a true philosopher with highly facile cross-over skills who can also be completely trusted in either camp.

When I sought such leaders for the research for this book, they were very hard to find. We can study model leaders like Stayer or Pat Kerrigan at General Motors, but each of their stories is very uniquely defined. The transition process at the financial services company began and ended so quickly and with such a clearly dangerous political aftermath, most leaders were reluctant to be aligned with any transition successes. Therefore, those who have shared their perceptions choose to be invisible. But they are alive. They do have remarkable leadership skills and have taken most of the best team practices underground and still use them to get the job done.

Philosophical Subversiveness

One common trait among effective transitional leaders is a sense of subversiveness about the power and potential of the new outcomes. A manager within one of my client companies described it as the ability to know who has the most to lose from a successful transition, and then finding ways to build alliances with those people. While this may sound duplicitous, I was struck by the fact that these transition managers had such clear faith in the new philosophy that they could establish alliances purely on the results and benefits for their resistant partners. Although the transition leaders often avoided quality jargon, as well as too much emphasis on the team process, they could sell the positive outcomes as something that the line people could use to bolster their reputation.

The leader also could use the results of a team initiative to gradually pull those alliances deeper into the philosophy. The key to success appears to be the intuitive ability to reveal the power of the results in response to the line partner's needs and ability to accept change. Many traditional hierarchic managers can be sold on results, and many of the effective leaders (not to mention all the TQM and reengineering vendor's salespeople) know to sell the results harder than the process or philosophy.

Team Transference

Another characteristic among most leaders I viewed was the ability to watch the development of a TQM team and gauge that development to the environment outside the team. Many leaders worked hard to keep their teams sequestered during the initial stages of development. The leader's focus was also on keeping the team's energy channeled exclusively on team behavior rather than encouraging premature transfer of new skills and practices back to the old system. Outsiders were carefully briefed by team leaders before they were allowed to watch team meetings and teams were often cautioned to not offer too much detail to the outside world about the work and development of the team; the leader kept the team developmental progress firmly underground.

This awareness of the developing energy of the team, and it's potentially threatening impact on those outside the team, also became a deliberate part of the team development. Teams were taught that "everybody else may not understand what is happening to us" and because the eventual outcome of the team's work would require outside acceptance, the team must manage the "marketing" of their process very carefully. In several cases this idea of "our little secret" served as an additional motivator in the establishment of a team identity.

The advice I received from leaders who had successfully avoided this communication obstacle was to encourage their teams to sell the results and outcomes of the process without any attempt to sell the unique process the team used. After the results were evident to people outside the team, then the team could safely share the interaction experience they found so exciting.

Results as the Commodity of Exchange

The successful leaders whom I interviewed often expressed a concept which demonstrates the delicate balance between work inside and outside the team. Many said that they learned this lesson the hard way, by doing it wrong first and having to repair the damage. Often, newly formed teams, when properly led, develop a powerful sense of excitement about their personal growth and developing capabilities. They often develop a zealousness about their new found inspiration and want badly to communicate this zeal to the uninitiated. They are far less concerned with where the uninitiated's perceptions are when they deliver the good news because they feel that their message is so powerful that it simply doesn't matter what others feel.

The danger here is inherent. Not only do these highly motivated team members not get the reaction they expected, the reaction they do get will ultimately reduce the chances of a successful transfer of improvements to the line operators. The leaders who explained this process of destructive outcomes had the same solution. *Sell the results instead of the power of the process.* If the suggested changes are effective at improving the end process, then it is not difficult to express exactly how those changes will make the work easier or provide them with better illumination from senior management or whatever indication of value the person needs to see personal accomplishment. Results as the commodity of exchange is almost a universally acceptable way to open a dialogue about change. Effective leaders know to expect and deal with the natural resistance to change and to channel that resistance into a personal "what's in it for you" message that doesn't shut down further communication. While this seems rather basic, the key point is to rely on this simple concept and to try not to market the team's personal growth excitement as the primary commodity of exchange.

This is difficult because the team excitement is so loud and powerful, and often the psychology of the leader is based on his or her desire to have that excitement generated in the first place. In other words, the team feels good about it's developmental growth, and the leader feels good that they feel good. The hard part for leaders is to remember that those feelings don't matter much to those outside the team and may even be perceived as elitist, which will ultimately ruin the operational outcomes for everyone.

The next major area related to team-to-line transfer requires the leader to project the most likely outcomes for the team. The leader then must identify line managers who will be affected by those outcomes far before they are evident to anyone else. In many cases, leaders knew where the real behavior changes would be well before they were visible to team members. Sometimes this was easy. In the case of teams working on processes within one department, the department manager was involved as a consultant from the start of the project and occasionally served as the team's sponsor. In more cross-functional cases this arrangement was not so easy for leaders to project. Building alliances early in the process may be an art form more than a learned skill, but several managers I have worked with identified this area as a key requirement.

When Pat Kerrigan of General Motors took over a huge parts plant that was given up for dead by senior management, she demonstrated effective behaviors from the outset. Instead of sequestering herself with P&Ls or creating a team to study problems, she did two completely unheard of things. First, Kerrigan walked throughout the plant for three full weeks meeting workers, some who had never even seen their plant managers before, and said to them, "Hi! I'm Pat Kerrigan. Do you think we can make this place work or not?"

Kerrigan then involved the union in every key senior management decision. She opened the books for them to see how serious the financial situation was and told them that the only solution to saving union jobs was to turn around the procedures and operations of the plant. The memorable quote from the senior union leader in the plant was: "Pat Kerrigan ain't got a phony bone in her body."

Pat knew where the crunch behavior was going to come from and started there. She also spoke to people in terms from their value system, not her own. Once she developed an alliance with people, she was free to offer changes that would have previously been rejected out of hand.

Leading the Roll-Out Process

The team's improvements to an operational system now must be rolled out to become a permanent part of the business operation. The use of all the skills that the leader has developed must drive the process of final transfer. Leaders must be able to think beyond the needs of their team both individually and collectively. They must concentrate almost exclusively on the needs of the permanent operators and their management. When the spotlight comes on they know it should illuminate the line performers and their managers, and that team members need to remain behind the scenes ensuring the success of others.

The payoff for the team members comes from the realization that their solutions are working well, and that they have accomplished their task. The payoff for line operators not on the team comes from the benefits of the new process, and the rewards available to them from improved output.

Shifting the emphasis from the team to the line does not mean that the leader abandons the team. On the contrary, the leader's sensitivity to team issues and emotions is a vital part of the continuation of the team. The last step in effectively leading a TQM or reengineering transition is giving support to the team members as the team disbands to ensure that each member perceives the improvement personally. This allows the organization to derive maximum benefit from the team members' newly acquired skills. Here the leader works tirelessly to lobby for team members to secure new assignments and see that they are never punished for having served on the team. The leader becomes an agent for the members' continued opportunity to grow and contribute to the organization. This requirement for leaders can be very difficult, especially if there is no real buy-in to the new process. In that case, the leader's skills at counseling individuals to help them find a way to cope with the feelings of loss and frustration and to find a way to perform as positive contributors must be effectively demonstrated.

I was surprised when I discovered that disbanding teams sometimes contained members who felt that they simply could not return to the old world of hierarchy. Those people for whom the process was a highly personal growth experience — often the first such growth experience in their work lives — found the changes too powerful to ignore and could not return to a world that did not support further development and often rejected the newly found skills. Leaders who were not ready for this possibility were often depressed by the loss of these team members. Those who were aware of the possibility were sometimes able to assist individual team members with other opportunities, either in other companies or elsewhere in the same company. If senior management was not completely aware of the process they were about to unleash, the higher turnover could become an undesirable but likely outcome.

In an example from my work, the ten most senior leaders of a foundry had attended an Outward Bound event and were transformed into a tightly joined team. They approached me and asked me to design a similar event for the next tier of managers, the middle- and first-line supervisors. They also wanted the supervisors to return from the experience with solid methods and initiatives to join with the senior team to form one cohesive management team.

The results of the experience surprised everyone, especially me. During the outdoor experience, I insisted on a regular rotation of leadership assignments as each new group task was given. Once we got to the woods, the group simply counted off as they stood in a circle. Each consecutive task was led by the next person in order. The last task they received at the end of their three-day program was led by the least senior, least experienced supervisor on the team. He had only been appointed supervisor six weeks before the training. The assignment given to this motivated leader was to lead the team to design and implement a transfer project that would not be implemented until they returned to the foundry. The dual purposes of this project were to, first, bind the supervisor's team to the senior team in a seamless fashion, and second, to resolve a longstanding production problem that had been previously identified by both teams before the training. This assignment was the most demanding of any assignment the team had attempted previously and by traditional standards, the man leading the assignment was the least well equipped to do so.

Almost immediately, the group chose to return with a concrete plan to reduce the foundry scrap rate in a significant way. The scrap-rate situation had been a serious problem for years, and so far no solution had ever had a longlasting effect. The supervisors felt that if they had complete buy-in to a plan from the management team they could permanently change the wasteful processes. In addition to all the technical planning they did, they also came up with some simple and highly effective ways to bond with the senior team. The common sense leadership ability that this inexperienced supervisor demonstrated throughout this process was absolutely inspiring. He listened, summarized, questioned, challenged, and supercharged his team to return to the foundry and get the job done. He never lost sight of the interpersonal task the team faced and constantly challenged the team to think about how the senior team would relate to their plans.

Three weeks after they returned, the scrap rate had already fallen 12% and within two months it had fallen 42%, where it remained for several months while new production systems were designed and implemented. The pride among the management team was evident on everyone's face. They couldn't wait to show me their results, and I couldn't wait to see them. It made great sense that the presentation they had prepared was led by our young task leader. He was nervous, but still did a great job in showing his audience what they accomplished.

After the presentation was over, I was sitting discussing the whole process with Ernie, the plant manager. Ernie was an old-school foundryman, raised in foundries with adversarial union relationships, likely to curse out a poor performer in public, and generally a tough customer who led through a position of punitive power. The team-led empowerment process that he had recently been part of had affected him profoundly. But old thought processes change slowly and he was prone to lapse back to old behaviors occasionally. As we sat in his office he spoke in his normal foundry volume (lots of foundry men are nearly deaf and talking to them is sometimes humorous as they literally scream calmly at you). He was casually remarking that now that they'd gotten these "young bucks" on board with correct new behaviors and his job was to find ways to keep them that way. As he offered this idea, the leader who had just successfully made the presentation, was walking by Ernie's office and overheard the sentiment Ernie expressed. He stopped, paused, came back to the open door and said: "No Ernie, my motivation is not your job or your problem. Your job is to provide us with resources and guidance as we carry out our plans and then get out of our way and let us get them done. Do that and we'll all get rich together."

He delivered this clarifying thunderbolt with neither rancor nor malice, but as a simple statement of fact. After he said it he smiled and walked away. Ernie turned to me, grinned and said, "Six months ago I'd have fired him for that, now I might see if there's something I've done recently that got in his way, and if not then forget about it. If we ever went back to the old way of doing business, we'd lose him and a dozen others just like him."

That little slice of life in an effective team environment remains clear in my mind. This example illustrates that for a worker to rejoin the old world once they have experienced the personal growth potential of an empowered workforce is simply regression. Effective leaders of the transition process know this intuitively.

This scenario illustrates the evolutionary nature of transitions. Once the team is capable and willing to accept full responsibility for its intended outcomes, the process by which they are achieved is up for grabs. Leaders need to allow the teams the leeway, experimentation, and the room to think "outside the box" to arrive at creative and effective decisions.

I recently interviewed a human resource manager in a relocation service company about his transition team charged to implement a team empowered operating philosophy. He said the team was not aware that they were working on "anything like TQM stuff." They thought they were simply looking at ways to streamline decision making within the company and believed that empowered teams was the best way to accomplish that end. They were working at their own pace and designed their own approach. The manager I spoke with was involved only as a resource and an occasional reminder that they needed to keep to their own preset deadlines. It was an effective transition process unlike any other I had seen before, particularly in its lack of structure and pressure.

It is important to realize that sometimes a transition might not be a good idea; it simply might not work. There are certain requirements that need to be met before the concept can make sense to its players, and every organization isn't ready for the change. If the transition is allowed to create its own evolutionary energy, then it will test its own readiness in a far more effective way than traditional management could devise.

Conclusions

An extension of the lesson that an effective transition to a team-centered, operator-level decision-making philosophy often results in changes which cannot translate compatibly to old hierarchic concepts is seen in the personal outcomes of the leaders of such transitions. Successful transition leaders are often permanently changed through the experience. They develop nearly obsessive resistance to autocratic decision making. They end up believing fervently the quote from Ralph Stayer, "It is immoral to be a leader of a organization today and not allow people to develop to their fullest." They have exceptionally high standards for performance and know that their role is to coach and guide others to achieve the absolute best they can produce. They are excited about improvement and that excitement pervades everything they do at work. Because the hierarchic world from which they came is often suffering from poor performance, these successful leaders simply don't fit back in the old world. If the company isn't truly committed to continuing the transition, the most effective transition leaders probably will not remain there.

A further extension of this incompatible outcome for transition leaders is that their team members feel it too. Effective leadership spawns effective leaders. That rule of work still remains the same. Successful leaders develop a nearly automatic role of mentor to new developing leadership. Organizations need to realize that the post-transition process can be risky if the team is not adequately challenged and allowed to continue their development. The worst-case scenario often includes teams of empowered people leaving one company and moving collectively to another, sometimes to a direct competitor. However, it is possible if we add another skill to the list for effective leaders to avoid that worst-case scenario. When leaders are effective at managing upward, either through subtle guidance of their managers or through more confrontative skills like those demonstrated by my team-leader friend in the foundry, then the transition can continue smoothly. New developing leaders can be challenged with new assignments while existing leaders can serve in the roles of coach and mentor.

The ability to manage upward in this particular application can sometimes become very demanding for transition leaders. Often senior management feels fear and confusion about their own roles in the developing new world and those emotional reactions result in very difficult behavior. Skills more related to clinical counseling and psychology may be required to help these managers remain confident as the transition continues. The example of Ernie, in the previous story, demonstrates the emotional pain that senior managers may experience throughout this process. The ability of team leaders to help them through that experience can be vital in keeping the momentum flowing.

Chapter Six will examine the synthesis of all the transition factors and put them into a sequence of broadly stated steps for leaders to follow. These steps represent a culmination of the detailed messages covered thus far and are designed to serve as a checklist for transition leaders.

SIX

A Checklist for Leading Transitions

Throughout this work I have stressed that the essence of effectively managing a transition to empowered team practices from a hierarchy requires a unique blend of technical and interpersonal knowledge, skills, and techniques. I have suggested that much of that blend is likely to be intuitive on the part of effective leaders. I doubt that a completely effective training program could be designed that would adequately prepare a leader to bridge the gap between the two incompatible philosophies related to the role of employees in decision making.

This chapter represents what I have gleaned from reading, interviewing, leading transition teams, coaching others who have led teams, and observing what seems to work. I have seen more transition failures than successes, and I believe that the failures often were the result of an approach which concentrated too heavily on either the technical or the interactive side. What follows is a series of sequential steps which represent the most essential mileposts to lead a longlasting, productive transition to a team-centered operation.

The steps are designed to provide a general direction on the transition journey and also allow enough leeway to arrange as many side trips as the travelers require. The intent here is to provide leaders with a behavioral balance among the following three general objectives:

1. A solid structural approach to empowered problem solving, based on data, research, and a clear sense of intended outcomes.

2. A clear understanding of and a motivation to capture the value of empowered teamwork, with incrementally increased levels of freedom for teams to make their own decisions with full authority and accountability.

3. A strong sense of the impact of the team's performance on the parent organization, in terms of the effect on non-team performers and team members.

One additional note is required before leaders charge off to lead transitions. There are 15 steps in this plan. They take a long time to complete, almost always longer than planned. A 15-step model is educationally weak as a way for people to direct their own behavior, let alone others. So leaders are strongly encouraged to subdivide these steps into groups of four or five items. It is also unwise for leaders to view these steps as isolated initiatives. The steps are all related to each other and often the significance of any one of them hinges on the requirements of another.

One way to use these steps is to view them as guideposts and general direction setters. A leader who is well into a transition assignment might find them useful as checkpoints to be sure that he or she is thinking about the right stuff and covering the important bases. They might also serve a leader whose project is stuck or bogged down by way of diagnosis about essentials.

15 STEPS TO LEADING A SUCCESSFUL TRANSITION INITIATIVE

1. Develop a collaborative, investigative relationship with project sponsors to ensure uniform understanding of the initiative's intended outcomes. Develop a broad-based communication plan for members of the organization with different subsets for different groups, depending on their involvement in the transition.

2. Use the collaborative relationship with sponsors to select a core team for the project. Choose team members as much for interpersonal skills as technical skills. Choose team ability over individual contribution potential.

3. Once a core team is assembled, working jointly with the sponsor(s), give the team its charge in the broadest of messages, without solution examples. Keep the charge focused on clear outcomes rather than the processes or procedures needed to achieve them. Coach the team to operate the communication plan.

4. Lead the team's developmental process. Lead the team to establish behavioral ground rules, agreed norms, values, and conflict resolution techniques.

5. Lead the team to focus on a specific improvement target, not immediate solutions. Begin contact with management of line areas affected by the focused target process. Encourage line managers and operators to visit the team and view their progress.

6. Influence the team to work exclusively with facts and data collected about the current situation, and lead them to arrive at probable causes of the problem situation.

7. Lead the team to create possible improvements to the process most closely related to the probable causes. Insist that they develop several possible improvements. Insist that all conclusions be supported by factual data.

8. Facilitate (not lead) the group to recreate their best improvement idea in pilot test format, with a full roll-out to follow.

9. Use the collaborative relationship between the line organization affected by the change and the team to facilitate buy-in. Influence an increase in the alliance strength between line operators and pilot designers.

10. Once the pilot is ready to run, coach team members to let go of control positions and move to secondary positions as consultants and experts.

11. Begin a collaborative approach to managers of team members to ease their impending reentry back to previous assignments. Coach team members to prepare a reentry plan with their original department managers.

12. Provide resources for the pilot test and eventual full roll-out. Use sponsor collaboration to free up needed resources.

13. Facilitate new team leadership (emerging from team membership) to review pilot data and plan full roll-out details. Facilitate a full presentation by the team to their sponsor.

14. After roll-out transfer to line organizations, disband team, concentrating on uncertainty and morale issues for team members. Rely on team members' managers to assist in the transition.

15. Debrief entire process with sponsor. Accept new assignment (start at Step 1).

The following summaries may help in clarifying the outcome of each step.

Step 1

Develop a collaborative, investigative relationship with project sponsors to ensure uniform understanding of the initiative's intended outcomes. Develop a broad-based communication plan for members of the organization with different subsets for different groups, depending on their involvement in the transition.

Too often leaders of sponsored projects view the assignment as a sort of vision quest given to them by the elders of the tribe. They seldom question the assignment or make any real effort to understand the situation which the project solves or improves. In my work training managers on the basics of project management, even prior to the use of TQM/reengineering philosophies, it would surprise me to see the managers resist the idea that effective project leadership included copious communication with project sponsors about the need for the project. Often the prevailing message from managers was that questioning the sponsor about the rationale for the assignment would be viewed as a lack of commitment or fear of failure. There simply is no reasonable position between sponsors and project leaders that does not include a fully collaborative approach. Since the transition process requires that the leader be clear about the outcomes rather than the processes of achieving those outcomes (which is the responsibility of the new team), he or she must be acutely aware of the bigger picture in which the project is positioned. Throughout the initiative, the project leader will need to be in constant communication with the sponsor for a myriad of purposes, not the least of which is constant validation or refocusing of the project outcomes.

One effective way for team leaders to test their own

understanding and the sponsor's clarity is through the development of an organization-wide communication plan. As this plan is agreed upon, issues of trust and information flow must be agreed upon as well.

Step 2

Use the collaborative relationship with sponsors to select a core team for the project. Choose team members as much for interpersonal skills as technical skills. Choose team ability over individual contribution potential.

New team leaders often have told me that one of their biggest mistakes early on in the project was to select their teams in too much detail too soon. The idea of developing a core of key team members who could work closely together in the initial stages of the project made a great deal more sense. As the focus of the initiative developed though communication with the sponsor and team leader, the team could best decide what additional human resources were necessary to add to the team. They could also decide to what degree those resources are needed to be committed (e.g., full-time, part-time, as advisors). If the leader's job is to develop a team that is willing to fully own the problem-solving process they are beginning, it makes good sense not to over-select the team players. In addition, to have a primary core of well informed team members facilitates the leader's desire to provide an opportunity for new leaders to emerge.

The other big mistake which leaders helped me identify consisted of choosing team members from a purely technical or task-oriented vantage point, as opposed to looking at the interpersonal potential. This was especially true on projects whose needs for data collection and analysis led them to recruit IS experts who traditionally worked in individual contributor roles. Not uncommonly these people were naturally resistant to the team empowerment concept and sometimes lacked adequate interpersonal communication skills. The requirement for leaders and sponsors at the initial stages of the project is to choose a core of team members who have good technical analysis skills and a predisposition to work in a team format, with demonstrable skills in both areas.

Step 3

Once the core team is assembled, together with the sponsor(s), give the team its charge in the broadest of messages, without solution examples. Keep the charge focused on clear outcomes rather than processes needed to achieve them. Coach the team to operate the communication plan.

This concept has been most eloquently popularized by Peter Senge in his lectures and book *The Fifth Discipline*. He offers the example of Japanese leaders in the role as the visionary direction-setters for their corporations. Their behavior, says Senge, consists of gathering their key operations people and offering only the vaguest information about new directions for the company. They speak of outcomes in the broadest terms and shy away from specific behavioral examples. The motive for this technique should be obvious to proponents of empowered team decision making. The actual behaviors of working within their organizations belong to the operators and not to senior leaders. The truly effective directions for the organization come best from the people who actually make them happen. This concept can and does translate easily to the role of leaders in American companies who are in the initial stages of TQM initiatives, and who seek to develop empowered teams to get the job done. Leaders who can provide a general direction for the newly formed core team enable that team to explore a greater range of solutions to the problems they seek to fix. When this subtle skill is used with new teams, the leader may need to use the strong collaborative role with the sponsor to refocus the entire project, as a result of the creative processes the team may devise.

I have seen such a redirection of the original charge accomplished very effectively once the team had done a bit of research into the assumptions on which the original project was based. In an example mentioned earlier, a team was originally charged with the assignment to change mail service vendors to lower costs. Initial research did validate that costs were way out of line. The reason why was more related to the system in place for using the service rather than a lack of vendor performance. Once the sponsor was presented with the team's initial research data, he refocused the team's charge to reduce the cost of the service rather than tell them how to do it. The result of the project lowered the cost past his yearly targets in just six weeks and the savings are still rolling in.

Step 4

Lead the team's developmental process. Lead the team to establish behavioral groundrules, agreed norms, values, and conflict resolution techniques.

My experience and research indicate that many leaders not only do not understand and embrace this responsibility, they overtly avoid it. The interactive dynamic of a forming functional team is a complex process and requires a knowledge set lacking throughout most of corporate America. Once leaders realize the potential for group cohesion as a result of this step and the certainty that the group can solve its own interpersonal conflicts, it is not uncommon for the leader to bring in team-building experts to help in the accomplishment of this step. The point here is that the group developmental process is far more powerful than any of the technical requirements the leader may impose. The group will develop independently of the leader. When leaders accept that inevitability they will recognize their responsibility to guide the process to better accomplish team goals effectively and efficiently.

Step 5

Lead the team to focus on a specific improvement target, not immediate solutions. Begin contact with management of line areas affected by the focused target process. Encourage line managers and operators to visit the team and view their progress.

The intent here is to resist the team's natural hierarchical behavior of solving the problem as soon as they think they know what it is. Those behaviors have been rewarded for employees throughout their careers and often it takes a great deal of energy for leaders to help teams get past the quick-fix mentality. Because the practice to encourage is to look more at the process than the problem outcome, the need for teams to gather detailed data about the current situation is a necessity for the project to be based on solid assumptions. This insistence on fully measuring the current situation also serves as an important psychological tenet for the newly developing team. The power of the team should be based on a clear need to get tasks completed effectively. Effective teams need to have worthwhile tasks to complete to feel a true sense of team accomplishment. This spirit is exemplified when, for example, the remaining crews of battleships and other military groups meet yearly since World War II. The teamwork that was achieved on those ships still holds their members together despite nearly 50 years in which the team did not behaviorally exist. Those members will proudly tell anyone who asks that their work together was clear, everyone knew exactly what their job was, and the outcomes were definitely important in the greater effort of the war. The idea that they are all friends or all love each other simply isn't relevant compared to the reason they were formed in the first place.

In the lighter example of our newly formed problem-solving teams, the discipline required to establish a factual basis for all the team's behavior accomplishes a similar outcome. It prevents interpersonal differences from interfering in the teams' work and keeps the team focused on a target bigger than the members' personal agendas.

There are several behaviors which are vital for leaders and which are not indicated in these steps because they appear as support behaviors in all of the steps. Among those behaviors is the alliance-building that the leader needs to initiate with groups that eventually will be affected by the team's work. As the team begins to focus its attention on specific processes to improve, the leader needs to establish sound relationships with line managers to more easily facilitate the changes coming downstream. The creation of these alliances as early as possible is a behind-the-scenes obligation of the leader. The leader will also need to nurture the alliances throughout the process and even after projects are completed in consideration of future requirements.

Step 6

Influence the team to work exclusively with facts and data collected about the current situation and lead them to arrive at probable causes of the problem situation.

Step 7

Lead the team to create possible improvements to the existing process most related to the probable causes. Insist that they develop several possible improvements.

Much of the current literature related to leading new processes is centered around these steps as the essence of the experience. They are the core of the technical aspect of transition leadership, and to minimize them would certainly result in the ultimate failure of the project. The key element is the intuitive requirement for the leader to use the developing technical capability of the team as an opportunity to move gradually away from the center and to allow new leaders to take over direction of the group process. This also helps to free up the leader to create the necessary bridges to the outside world where the team's results will ultimately rest. Leaders I have interviewed about this requirement of intentional movement to the periphery of the team process say that it is extremely difficult to achieve. They spoke about how the seductive power of the team and the sense of excitement that now pervades the team's work are a powerful magnet to them. Added to this resistance to leave the team is often the realization that this power was a goal of the leader from the start and that it now exists so clearly within the team.

Step 8

Facilitate (not lead) the group to recreate their best improvement idea in pilot test format with a full roll-out to follow.

Step 9

Use collaborative relationships between the line organization affected by the change and the team to facilitate buy-in. Influence an increase in the alliance strength between line operators and the team pilot designers.

While these steps could easily fall into the previous description, they do have important elements in them which Steps 5, 6, and 7 do not. Notice that Step 8 states that the leader should facilitate and not lead the pilot design and the full organizational roll-out. The distinction between facilitating and leading for the team leader is based on the new leadership roles that often emerge from within the group. If the leader has selected the right people from the start and coached them through the proper developmental process, he or she should not lead in this step. To do so deprives the new leaders of an opportunity for success. Throughout these middle steps the original team leader has been gradually shifting roles toward a less central identity within the team and these steps allow that shift to continue. From the facilitator's role, the formal leader can protect emerging leaders from inexperienced mistakes yet still allow them to grow into the role. The concept of the pilot test also provides the team with a second chance before full roll-out.

Step 10

Once the pilot is ready to run, coach team members to let go of control and move to secondary positions as consultants and experts.

If the previous steps have gone as planned, now the team leader can find the time and resources to cement the team and the line organization together. As a coach, the leader's job is to help the team shift the control of the project to the operators who will actually make it go. The leader will have modeled behaviors of coaching and teaching that the team members can use to guide them through their new role as teachers and trainers to line operators. In many ways the original team leader and the manager(s) of the implementation line area become co-leaders of the project.

Step 11

Encourage team members to begin thinking about their work life after the project. Begin a collaborative approach to managers of team members to ease reentry back to previous assignments. Coach team members to prepare a reentry plan with their managers.

A Checklist for Leading Transitions

Step 11 begins a subtle change in the role of the leader and eventually of the team itself that is often lost when transitions are studied. The typical focus on task completion often obscures the important change the team is undergoing. Now that the primary and visible work of the team is complete, the leader's job is to begin the formal task of dissolving the team. The dissolution of the team is important because the team members represent a resource to the organization of increased value. The process by which the team moves on to new assignments or back to old ones has a great deal to do with whether the organization will be able to utilize that increased value. As previously stated, this responsibility of the leader can become highly sensitive, political, and has the potential to destroy the motivation of the team members who are still high from their latest successes.

To begin this delicate transition, the leader often introduces questions and activities that force the team to think beyond the details of evaluating the pilot test or preparing for the roll-out. Any danger that these questions may distract the team from their immediate tasks is minimized by the powerful motivation, now a completely internal function of the team members, to carry their project successfully to the end.

The leader's objective is to lead team members to develop an introspective analysis about their own future and contributions to the company. The leader works in the initial role of counselor and coach. In many ways the requirement is career management for each individual team member.

As a continuation and extension of this step, the leader uses Step 11 to work with the original managers of team members to assure the transitions to their next assignments. From a formal point of view, the leader is required to contribute to the performance appraisal of the people who have worked on the team and to report to their managers in detail the various contributions of the team members. It is often during these evaluative discussions that the leader can communicate the more subtle messages of what to expect when the team member returns to previous assignments. Working as a liaison between the employee and the manager, the leader often can suggest ways for the manager to better utilize the employee's expanded skills as well as the motivation the team members often bring back with them.

The leader can sometimes use this dialogue with team members' traditional managers to suggest new assignments. Extending the discussion and suggestions to include the sponsor is also a valuable way for leaders to expand the potential of the strong collaboration they have developed with the sponsor.

For example, some of the members from the team mentioned earlier that revised the mail process have been moved to other places within their division to lead similar but smaller improvement processes. Many of those team members now have a public reputation for improving systems, and work in rotational assignments to that end. Several of them have moved into first-line supervision roles, combining the continued requirements to get the division work done with the fact that staff reductions have placed all the previous work processes under review.

Step 12

Provide resources for the pilot test and eventual roll-out. Use sponsor collaboration to free up needed resources.

The last formal requirement for the leader in the successful completion of the team's project is to provide all the resources needed to ensure a smooth and efficient roll-out. In this step, all the important relationships that the leader has carefully developed are used to provide resources to the operators and managers who are permanently changing the way they work. The effectiveness of those relationships is fully tested in this step. If the leader has been a constant source of useful information about the progress and value of the team's work to as many sources as possible, this step is not difficult. The discussion in the previous steps points out opportunities for leaders to facilitate the contribution of resources for the roll-out.

However, some of the team leaders I have interviewed had a great deal of trouble with this task. They stressed in the strongest of terms that if the leader has failed at the bridge-building process, then they can be faced with trying to transfer the improved process to lines that neither understand it nor are willing to expend resources to embrace it. The emotional pain that leaders experience, especially within the team, to have come this far and be unable to complete the project fully or with drastically reduced resources was highly impactful to some of the leaders I spoke to.

Step 13

Facilitate new team leadership (emerging from team membership) to review pilot data and plan full roll-out detail. Coordinate full presentation to sponsor by team.

Because this is the last official public act by the team, the leader's role is one of helping the team prepare for their presentation to the sponsor. The team should handle all the details of the presentation while the leader works both internally and externally to provide presentation coaching and other needed resources.

I have had the opportunity to see back-to-back presentations for sponsors, one presented exclusively by the leader with team support, the other presented by the team with the leader in the background. The impact on the sponsor and guests (which included the managers of team members) was profoundly stronger from the team presentation.

Step 14

After roll-out transfer to line organizations, disband team, concentrating on grief, uncertainty and morale issues for team members. Rely on team member's managers to assist in the transition.

This step is often a formality if the others have been carried out fully and effectively. It should not be skipped, however. Psychologically, team members need to feel that the project is over. They need to realize that the strength of the experience is still useful to them personally, and that is what they will take with them as they move on. The essence of the team will end except as a model and a memory for future projects.

This step often is incorporated into a closing team celebration at the termination of the roll-out. Leaders and team members need to invite as many outsiders to the celebration, such as sponsors, line managers, senior executives, press, and media, as appropriate. However, my experience with the termination of powerful groups indicates that sometime before, during, or immediately after the formal public celebration, the leader needs to sit together with the team and formally end their charge. I have designed and delivered several of these termination meetings for disbanding teams and they can be very powerful events. If each member has the opportunity to talk a bit about the experience from their own developmental viewpoint, to acknowledge the contributions of others to that development, and to express their feelings of satisfaction, then those team members are better prepared to move onward and continue contributing. It is sometimes surprising to leaders to realize that there is a grieving process that is healthy and functional for team members. Within

A Checklist for Leading Transitions

the grief is the prevailing feeling that the team has been successful and has done its job. Too often this step is eliminated as an unnecessary expense and interruption to the work at hand. The results of not allowing this ending process are powerful and negative, just as they are in other applications of the grieving process when people have not been allowed to "let go."

This step has been tacitly ignored by team leaders and senior managers in my observations and the results of ignoring it are not fully documented, mostly because I have not found an adequate example of the step having been completed.

Without this step, team members return to old assignments with a strong sense of regret that the project is over and that life won't be as exciting as it has been. I have observed that they often go through the grieving process anyway, except that without this step they grieve back on their old job. Their behavior is viewed negatively or suspiciously and often their performance suffers. When their line managers speak to them about their "bad attitude" it only reinforces their expectation that work won't be as much fun anymore.

I believe that the more successful the team experience has been for its members, the greater is the need to formally end and disband the team.

Step 15

Debrief entire process with sponsor. Accept new assignment (start at Step 1).

This step is required to complete the full cycle. Often a formality if the leader has communicated freely with the sponsor and others throughout the process, this step is simply the formal, documented debrief of the entire process. There is one key consideration within this step which leaders have brought to my attention, especially when the team's project represents a new experience within the parent organization. Leaders and sponsors need to remember that they are pioneers for other teams and that they should document as many details as possible. If the sponsor and leader have set up their responsibilities correctly from the beginning, then documentation is a fully functional part of the process. Leaders of the teams to follow have stressed that the pioneers cannot over-document their process.

Finally, the leader needs a transition period before moving to a brand new assignment with a newly forming team. Since patience was a major requirement for leaders in our start-up steps, the leader who is fresh from a long and recently completed initiative may need a period of readjustment to meet the demands of starting over.

Conclusions

It is necessary to stress here that these 15 steps do not proport to be the sum total of effective transition leadership. These steps are mileposts for leaders throughout their journeys to help them stay on a direct path that still includes the essential needs of the players involved. The intent is to assure that the interactive, interpersonal power of the process be acknowledged as an integral part of the experience. An observer of the team meetings of fully functional problem-solving or decision-making teams will hear members verbalize the relationship part of the experience before they acknowledge skills, tools, or methodology. The magic of the team process is wrapped in empowerment more than anything else. These steps are designed to fully develop that power as an equal companion to the new technology in problem solving which results from a solid TQM/reengineering approach.

… **SEVEN** …

Conclusions

Although actual documentation is difficult to find, I believe that more transitions fail in their first effort than are successful. Much has been written about the reasons why and theories range from purely technical analysis to purely esoteric. Generally, from my viewpoint of what really is significant in understanding why so many transition attempts fail, it boils down to six key explanations. There are countless other reasons specific to individual cases of failure, but even those may simply be viewed as variations of these basic reasons.

1. Lack of full understanding of the values, outcomes, and potential inherent in the power shift which the transition will accomplish.

2. Lack of a clearly designed communication plan for every part of the organization and the leadership skills to deliver the plan effectively.

3. Perhaps as an extension of the lack of the communication plan cited above is the lack of a detailed behavioral plan for the operators of new work processes.

4. Lack of personnel who have the necessary training and experience in the rigorous rigors of team problem solving and process improvement.

5. Lack of adequate balance in the leadership of the transition between business line issues and human resources concerns.

6. A lack of persistence to stay the course when problems arise or individual initiatives fail.

Failed Process Sequences

Too often organizations begin an exploration of the possibility of an operating philosophy shift for all the wrong reasons, seeking to find new easy ways to get rich or richer. They pull in vendors to lead the process who are willing to alter established protocols of effectiveness, when the customer demands it, merely to be able to stay in the game.

At the financial services corporation, for example, the amount of executive leadership involvement at the beginning of the process was far too light and incomplete to demonstrate true understanding from the top. Executive overviews of a program that, if successful, would change the very essence of work at this corporation cannot meet the demands of philosophical buy-in that must be in place for the process to be successful. Senior leaders were aware only that a big training effort was about to begin and that the content of the training seemed sound enough to raise profits. There was virtually no evidence that senior managers realized that they were funding and signing off on a total operational change and so the results could never be successfully achieved.

If transitions are to be successful, an immense amount of time and effort must be invested at the top. In addition, leaders need to be ready to face the fact that many of their managers will not be able to make the necessary personal changes to complete the shift. Perhaps the quietest fact about transitions is the heavy toll on management census. In addition to the reduced number of middle- and first-line supervisors needed once the process is in place, usually less than half the traditional number, the changes that the survivors must complete are substantial. Traditional sources of power must be abandoned and replaced with faith in the team to produce the necessary results. Power is shifted to groups rather than resting in highly placed individuals. Unless all the players are prepared for that inevitability, no transition will really flourish.

All of this leads to one conclusion. If transitions are to work smoothly and consistently, senior and executive managers need to fully understand the philosophy, clearly communicate that understanding, and model the behavior that they wish others to adopt.

Businesses Must Lead the Charge, Not Human Resources

Changing the work process is not exclusively within the scope of human resources departments, yet many companies seat the effort there. This is not to say that human resources departments do not have a vital role in the success of the operation. The point is to illustrate the marriage of technical and human considerations needed if the transition is to survive. But the center of the change process should be located at the business line because, ultimately, the core of the idea is all about results to the customers. It is the business objectives that drive the process and with which the HR department is used as a partner.

A more subtle indicator that the process belongs primarily to the business and not HR is that every company evolves its own sense of and practice for the new work processes. The transition must be closely aligned to business issues because it will develop its own personality and identity, composed of the accumulated personalities of the people involved. There really isn't a rule book that serves every company equally well. HR departments which have mistakenly accepted the leadership of the transition are often forced to work from predetermined transition formulas and practices. They are not close enough to the real behaviors used before the transitions or the new ones the transition will introduce.

The fact of the matter is that the process evolves once the operators are clear about the philosophies and expected outcomes. That evolution must be allowed to work its own way, ideally guided by savvy HR leaders in partnership with business leaders.

The conclusions presented here are not overwhelming surprises. I have not uncovered some obscure secret that represents the DNA of effective transitions. We have all known the true essence of the movement if we have experienced its power in action and that is the real message. A glance at the histories of unsuccessful transitions shows that the human interaction potential works either toward success or toward failure, but it is never neutral. It is clear that the important conclusions all relate to humans, not to systems, processes, or other technologies. So, for me, the list looks like the following:

1. All the process and technology reasons that transitions fail are merely symptoms of the fact that the

significant people did not know enough about the philosophical messages of empowerment.

2. The simple and awesome power of people working together effectively as teams with control over their work is a power that senior managers have either known about and feared or not known about at all. Limited knowledge about the power of people working together has resulted in significant historical failures in modern history, from the outcomes of two world wars to the demise of the Soviet Union. Transitions from autocratic, hierarchical control to team decision making at the operational level will fail if the leaders do not understand the fundamental philosophies they have unleased.

3. When leaders do not understand the power of the idea they wish to operationalize, then they will lead from a position of fear. Their fundamental assumptions about people, work, power, and success will all be placed in jeopardy and their behavior will demonstrate those fears.

   What if adults at work don't need supervision?

   What if adults at work can and will make excellent business decisions without highly specialized training or experience?

   What if the role of the people at the top is to facilitate the efforts of the people at the bottom, whose performance standards will be set by themselves, and whose performance is motivated by a desire to have their outcomes be valued rather than to ensure someone else's profits?

   These are questions that drive the fear response to the empowerment movement, and until leaders can embrace all the possible answers to these questions transitions will likely continue to fail.

4. The process of the change must demonstrate the change itself. Autocratically mandated transitions don't work unless the transition plan demonstrates a team-centered approach.

5. The human interactive component is easily the most powerful aspect of the transition and will overshadow all others including technology and systems analysis.

6. If outcomes are clearly communicated and successes are fully shared among the teams that contributed to them, results will exceed the most optimistic projections. If not, no adjustment to the plan or technical improvement will be enough to produce satisfactory results.

If this book helps the reader prepare for his or her role in a transition and provides some useful guideposts, its purpose will have been met. The ability to lead the transition is perhaps one of the most demanding requirements in organizations today. One thing is certain: those who attempt to lead an organizational transition from a traditional hierarchy to a high-performance workplace will be greatly enriched and permanently, positively changed by the experience, regardless of whether the organization has the courage and conviction to change.

Index

Acceptance philosophy, 38
Alliance-building, 93–94, 95–96
Assimilation movement, 24–25
Automation age, 23–24

Beals, Vaughn, 60
Behavior
   cultural diversity of workforce and, 28–29, 37
   discipline needed for team, 94
   executives as models for, 37
   lack of plan for, 104
   pilot testing for, 65
   resistance to change affecting, 9
Business/human resources balance, 104, 105–8

Chief executive officer (CEO) role, 14–15
Commitment needs, 14–16, 18, 42–43

Communication
  managers as liaison for, 36
  needs during transition, 46–50, 55–57, 61–62, 91, 103
  plan development and testing, 87, 89–90
  recursiveness in, 61–62
  skills training for, 49–50, 51–52
  within diverse work teams, 32–34, 36
Competition rules, 8
Cultural diversity. *See* Diversity

Debriefing process, 101–2
Decision making
  diversity of transition teams affecting, 26–27, 34
  hierarchy approach compared with TQM, 13
  Japan compared with U.S., 33
  by labor force, 69
  managers' commitment to power shift, 42–43
  middle management affected by, 35
  as team objective, 86
  values of, 63–64
Demographic issues, 24
Diversity, 23–39
  communication aspects of, 32–34
  employee training about, 26
  fear of, 36–39
  hierarchy and, 27–31
  liabilities of, 34–39
  problem-solving issues of, 29–30
  psychological issues for workers, 31–32
Documentation, 102

Effective Performance Discussions workshop, 27–29
Employees
  control needs of, 14
  involvement in company, 68–69
  manager interaction, 41, 69, 98
  performance obstacles, 2
  trust issues, 68
  see also Transition teams
Empowerment
  examples of, 70
  interpersonal factors in, 42–43

INDEX

as transition objective, 86, 107
for work teams, 31–32
Ethnic issues. *See* Diversity
Evaluation techniques, 54–55
Executives
    diversity issues and, 36–38
    interpersonal skills of, 49
    lack of understanding by, 19
    see also Management

Feedback, 29
Fifth Discipline, The (Senge), 32, 91
Financial Services Corporation (pseudonym), 16–19, 21, 61

General Motors parts plant, 75–76
Goals comparison, 12
Group interaction skills. *See* Interpersonal skills
Groups. *See* Transition teams

Harley-Davidson Company, 68–69
Hierarchical organizations, 8–9
    diversity in, 27–31, 34
    survival facts for, 11–14
    transitions in, 15
Human resources, 21, 41–57, 104, 105–8

Improvement target, 93–95
Interaction skills. *See* Interpersonal skills
Interpersonal skills, 41–57
    for group interaction, 46–54
    need to develop, 5, 70
    as team member quality, 90–91
    technical skills compared with, 64–70
    transition steps and, 43–45

Japanese business, 3, 33, 91
Johnsonville Foods, 19–22, 70

Kerrigan, Pat, 75–76

Labor force
    automation impact on, 23–24
    changes in, 9, 25

Labor force (*cont.*)
  decision making by, 69
  diversity in, 23–39
  empowerment of, 42–43
  role in hierarchical organization, 8
  technology skills needed in, 25
  see also Employees; Management; *specific positions*
Leadership Alliance, The (video), 60
Leadership roles
  business/human resources balance needed for, 104
  communication skills and, 47, 91
  decision making and, 35, 69
  diversity fears affecting, 36, 38–39
  interpersonal skills needed for, 41–42, 47–48, 70
  in Japan, 91
  profile of, 59–60
  as team coach, 91–92
  transitions creating confusion in, 4–5
  see also Executives; Management; Supervisors; Transition team leaders
Learning organization concept, 32–33
Line management and operators, 52–54, 75, 88, 95–96
Line organization, 7
Listening skills, 47, 49

Management
  commitment issues, 14, 42–43
  as communications liaisons, 36
  diversity issues, 27–28, 30–31, 35, 36
  employee interaction, 41, 69, 98
  job description and role of, 10, 11
  problem-solving by, 30–31
  training for, 7, 16, 68, 89
  transfer of initiative within, 52–54
  transition effects on, 35, 45, 69, 105
  see also Line management; Supervisors
Market place competition, 8
Matrix philosophy, 15
Middle management, 35, 69, 105
Military groups, 93–94
Modeling concept, 37
Motivation, 80
Multiculturalism. *See* Diversity

INDEX 113

Operators. *See* Line management and operators
Outward Bound program, 78–79

Parent organizations, 86
Parking places example, 42
Pay raise alternatives, 21
Performance appraisals, 97–98
Personal growth philosophy, 21
Personnel policies. *See* Human resources
Peters, Tom, 60
Philosophical subversiveness, 72–73
Pilot design and testing, 52, 65, 88, 95–96
Portuguese employees, 28, 30
Power shift. *See* Transitions
Problem solving
  advantage of diverse workforce, 29–31, 32–34
  empowerment factors, 86
  necessary team skills, 50–52, 87–88
Process improvement teams, 52–54
Product design teams, 54
PROGRESS program, 50–51
Project management. *See* Management
Project sponsors. *See* Sponsor role

Quality management. *See* Total quality management

Recursiveness, 61–62
Redirection, 92
Reengineering
  definition of, 10–11
  developing teams for, 50
  failure of, 14–16
  philosophy of, 60–70
  transition steps for, 43–45, 47
  see also Total Quality Management
Reentry plans, 96–97
Rewards basis, 8–9
Role plays, 27–28
Roll-out process, 76–81, 95–96, 98–100

Scrap-rate example, 79
Self-management, 68–69
Senge, Peter, 32–33, 91

Sponsors, 6, 44
  developing relationship with, 87, 89-90
  presentations to and debriefings of, 98-100
  redirection by, 91-92
Stayer, Ralph, 6, 19-20, 60
Storming phase, 49-50
Success as obstacle, 3-4
Supervisors
  diversity issues, 27-28, 35
  as managers, 35
  Outward Bound experience, 78-79

Taylor and Fenn quality teams, 42
Teams. *See* Transition teams
Technology
  communication importance in, 32-34
  interpersonal skills compared with, 64-70
  jobs for non-U.S. employees, 25-27
  skills needed for team membership, 90
Termination meeting, 100-101
Total Quality Management (TQM)
  approach to diversity, 33-34
  definition of, 10-11
  development of teams, 50-52
  failure of, 1, 14-19, 41-42
  interpersonal aspects of, 41-57
  labeling drawbacks, 9-10
  philosophy of, 60-70
  pilot testing by teams, 52
  problem-solving approach of, 29
  success of, 19-22
  survival facts for, 11-14
  as tool for organizational change, 9
  transition steps for, 43-45, 47
  see also Reengineering; Transition teams

Training
  for communications skills, 49-50, 51-52
  about diversity issues, 26
  lack of, 68, 104
  learning organization concept, 32-33
  manager-employee interaction and, 41-42

INDEX

    for managers, 7, 16, 68, 89
    pilot test phase of, 52–53
    reduction of, 68
    role in hierarchical organization, 8
    role in transition, 18
    video for, 60
Transitions
    CEO role in, 14–15
    checklist for, 85–102
    diversity impact on, 23–39
    evolutionary nature of, 80–81
    examples of, 4–5, 16–22, 68–69
    failures of, 1, 11, 16–19, 55–56, 103–8
    objectives of, 86
    participants' roles in, 5–8
    power shift in, 15
    steps, 43–45, 71–83
    technical vs. human interaction skills, 65–67
Transition team leaders
    alliance-building by, 93–94, 95–96
    avoiding destructive outcomes, 74–76
    checklist for, 85–102
    communication skills, 44–45, 47, 51–52, 55, 61–63, 91
    documentation by, 102
    evaluation techniques of, 55
    leadership guidelines, 71–83
    as manager-employee liaison, 97
    philosophical issues, 60–70, 72–73
    role of, 59–70
    roll-out process, 76–81, 95–96, 98–100
    sponsor presentation, 99–100
    team development, 73–74, 87, 92–93
    technical vs. interpersonal skills needed by, 44–45, 64–70
    training of, 51–52
    transition effect on, 81–83
Transition teams, 6–8
    balance with outside work, 74–76
    choosing members for, 87, 90
    communication training for, 49–50
    decision making by, 9–14, 34
    development of, 50–52, 64, 73–74, 87, 92–93
    disbanding of, 77–78

Transition teams (*cont.*)
  evaluation techniques of, 54–55
  examples of, 68–69
  hierarchy approach compared with TQM, 13
  improvement target, 93–95
  interpersonal skills needed for, 41–57, 90
  labor force diversity and, 26–27, 31–34
  redirection of, 92
  reentry plans for, 77–78, 97–102
  roles of, 20–21, 44–45
  successes of, 20–21, 77, 81–83
  values and beliefs of, 63–64, 76
  weaknesses and failures of, 17, 54, 77–78
Trust issues, 46–47, 68

United States
  decision making compared with Japan, 33
  hierarchical organizations, 8–9
  labor force assumptions, 25
  organizational changes needed, 9
  post-World War II business boom, 3–4

Value systems, 63–64, 76
Vendors, 15–16, 17–18

Windsor, Connecticut, 29–30
Workforce. *See* Labor force